CHURCH MUSIC
IN A
CHANGING WORLD

By the same author:

A Handbook of Parish Music (Mowbray)
Making Church Music Work (Mowbray)
Music and the Alternative Service Book – Editor
    (Addington Press – RSCM/Mowbray)
The Chorister's Companion – Editor (RSCM)
The Psalms – Their Use and Performance Today –
    Editor (RSCM)
The Church Musician as Conductor (RSCM)
The ASB Psalter and Canticles – Editor (Collins)

Church Music
in a
Changing World

by

LIONEL DAKERS

Director of the Royal School of Church Music

MOWBRAY
LONDON & OXFORD

Copyright © Lionel Dakers 1984

ISBN 0 264 66951 7

First published 1984
by A. R. Mowbray & Co. Ltd,
Saint Thomas House, Becket Street,
Oxford, OX1 1SJ

Printed in Great Britain by Richard Clay
(The Chaucer Press) Ltd, Bungay, Suffolk.

'As some to church repair,
Not for the doctrine, but the music there'

Alexander Pope: *Essay on Criticism*

CONTENTS

Certain abbreviations have been used. These include

BCP = Book of Common Prayer 1662
ASB = Alternative Service Book 1980
RSCM = Royal School of Church Music
SATB = the traditional choir of sopranos, altos, tenors
and basses for which much church music is written

Whenever the word organist is used this usually implies
organist and choirmaster (or choir director), as the same
person frequently combines both tasks.

INTRODUCTION

What follows in these pages is a gathering together of some of the experiences, observations, discussions and subsequent personal thoughts arising from my ten years as Director of the Royal School of Church Music. This has happened to coincide with a period during which both the Church and the world at large have experienced a series of unique changes – some would say eruptions of volcanic dimensions – in which the one has helped to influence and shape the other.

Much of what I have to say is coloured by the welter of relatively swift liturgical change of which The Alternative Service Book 1980 is the outcome. Because society and its attitudes are changing, the Church is also changing. This is a fundamental fact which we do not always willingly grasp or come to terms with.

I also happen to be in a unique personal position. Much of what I have observed has been as a member of the congregation, having previously been for most of my working life on the other side as an organist.

My work provides opportunities for discussion at all levels. This extends from archbishops to village clergy, from Free Church ministers to Roman Catholic cardinals, and from cathedral organists to reluctant organists, those splendid souls who contribute so much to the Church in a very special way.

All this, and more, I see in travels which take me from Aberdeen to Australia and from Hong Kong to Hereford. I have quickly learned that face to face discussion can be a revealing – and reliable – thermometer for finding out what makes people tick.

Although this book is directed mainly towards Anglicans, its substance can just as easily apply to other denominations, all of whom without exception have experienced change. I find I have learned much from what the other denominations have to offer, not least what we have in common rather than what separates us.

Foremost in all this are the problems, the challenges and – let us not underestimate it – the joys of new thinking which have helped to stimulate the current reshaping of our worship patterns and the resulting musical issues. All in all, I believe we live in exciting times.

The changing world and the changing Church do not necessarily imply a need to abandon proven and valid traditions. Far from it. This is one of the mistakes sometimes arrogantly linked with certain aspects of renewal thinking.

After three hundred years of near predictability in the Anglican Church, and because the comparatively recent changes have been traumatic in the extreme, it is understandable that we are to a certain extent still fumbling in the dark. Because of this, many clergy are groping for new ideas and new expressions of worship, knowing only too well that both are needed. Maybe some have returned from a conference bubbling over with enthusiasm for putting into practice ideas they have picked up. But fervour has its dangers; for innovation which moves too quickly, especially against a conservative and fairly static background such as the Church of England, can burn itself out without having a chance to develop and grow rationally.

Because today it is fashionable to question virtually everything, especially within the orbit of what is loosely termed 'the establishment', we do not always stop to think whether what we have in mind, not least musically, may necessarily be right for us in our Utopian quest.

Church musicians are sometimes taken for granted and

their work only commented on, and usually adversely, when things go wrong. By the reverse token, musicians do not always consult with or work with their clergy as readily as they might. Is it to be wondered at that suspicions, threats and jealousies, be they real or imaginary, result?

A sizeable part of this book is devoted to clergy/organist relationships, the root of much that is discreditable in the Church, though it can equally be a source of many good things. The inevitability of music is inescapable within the context of worship, but using it to advantage for evangelistic purposes is another matter.

I have therefore tried to offer some guidelines, while at the same time endeavouring to understand the legitimate claims of all sides. My wish is to help in all situations, and never to inflame. In doing just this I have drawn on and quoted, with or without acknowledgement, chance comments made either in my hearing or by people I have been in discussion with and whose viewpoint I felt to be pertinent.

I have no doubt that in this book, as so often in my work, I shall probably be preaching more to those who are converted and committed to the cause of music in worship than to those who question its validity and its power, and who sometimes seem to draw conclusions which might be considered to be destructively critical.

I make no excuse for reiterating much that I may have said before in books or articles. The fact is that these things need to be said again and again.

1

SETTING THE SCENE

Although the revision of liturgies, services, even complete prayer books, is as much an ongoing process today as it has been on and off for more than three hundred years, the past thirty years have been a particularly active era in this respect. All of us, whatever our denomination and wherever we may happen to live, are only too aware of this and of the prominence it has attracted.

There is of course a parallel here with the secular world where we have probably seen more change in the past thirty years or so than in the whole of the preceding three hundred. Enormous advances have been made, and made very swiftly, in science, electronics, computers, medicine, space travel and jet travel, much of which has made the dreams and predictions of H. G. Wells and George Orwell something of a reality.

In society at large we are all caught up in a changing world, whether or not we wish to be. While much of the change is for the better, some is sinister, with a foreboding which warns that while we now have great and hitherto unharnessed power at the mere flick of a switch, much could all too easily go very wrong. Nevertheless, it is a fact that virtually every aspect of society the world over has been affected and influenced by change in our time.

The Church, with a capital 'C', is not exonerated from change – and why should it be? If the Church elects to opt out and live, as some of us all too readily would, in a private and closeted society where the past is all that really matters, then we shall not only be living in a make-believe world but shall have contributed in no uncertain way towards a stagnation which at worst can only spell decay and ultimately annihilation. Change need not automatically be equated with the decay which Lyte envisaged in his hymn, 'Abide with me'.

I believe that through one of the many manifestations of the Holy Spirit in our day and age, in this instance we have been reminded that now is the moment to think *how* we worship and what words we use. We have suddenly, or relatively suddenly, woken up to this realization; but, as with all reawakenings, it can easily overspill into excesses, either in encouraging us to dig our toes more than ever into the past or to bring out a surfeit of, for want of a better word, enthusiasm. Of the two, the latter is the more dangerous for, although it may seem to be the more exciting, it can quickly get out of control.

In a nutshell, we are experiencing a liturgical revolution, even if it is a relatively painless one. Nevertheless, this is not without a certain element of writing on the wall, which is the *raison d'etre* of this book and our point of departure.

The excitement, as I see it and will constantly try to show in what follows, is all part of the process and, more to the point, of the challenge which I believe is ours within the Church. How we elect to play this challenge is another matter.

What has resulted in the Church of England and in much of the Anglican Communion is not so much something new as a rethinking of existing material. The problem is that the ASB, even if it is a convenient gathering up under one cover of material which had mainly been in use for some time, is still thought of in many quarters as new and therefore, by implication, suspect. It is, after all, the first major new Anglican prayer book to have appeared in England in more than three hundred years.

Much of what I want to say, although of necessity slanted towards Anglican worship patterns, is in no way

5

exclusive. We are constantly seeing that where doctrine and theology separate the denominations, and will probably continue to do so for the foreseeable future, music speaks a common language which allows few denominational barriers.

Nor would I suggest that this book is only for those who use the ASB. As we now have an alternative prayer book it is obvious that we should discuss the new more than merely reiterate what has been written in the past about the BCP. My personal affection for the BCP is in no way diminished, though I have to confess that having widely experienced the ASB I now find Cranmer's language hard to use in the context of public worship, and especially in the Holy Communion service.

I think there is also a danger of the BCP becoming a refuge of convenience for what some see as 'the stormy blast'. The fact that in a rapidly changing world some find the BCP the last bastion of ecclesiastical tradition is fair enough. It would also seem to indicate that there is ample room for both the old and the new. The unique, not antique, flexibility of Anglican worship allows every persuasion of churchmanship within that denomination to flourish without let or hindrance. This in itself is quite something.

Whatever the end product, how dull it would be if uniformity, which is not by any means the same as unity, prevailed. Where we have succeeded in moving together is in the adoption of a number of common texts, the result being that the major denominations the world over are now sharing certain texts. Would that this, in an avowedly ecumenical age, could bring us more together in terms of the music, for here we have one of the most sensitive, even divisive, areas to have emerged.

Having said this, I do not for one moment believe that any musical divisions, many of which will be discussed in the ensuing pages, are merely the result of the ASB, though this may have been a contributory factor. I am convinced that many of the differences we are currently experiencing in terms of types of music, spring from far deeper and more fundamental problems which will be discussed as we go along. Human nature being what it is, strange and unpredictable things can result.

WHAT THE CHANGES HAVE RESULTED IN

Although the changes as such will be discussed in the next chapter, we should perhaps first see something of what these changes have brought about.

(a) The Eucharist

The most immediate reality is the all but universal move in the Anglican Church towards eucharistic worship as the focal point in the life and witness of many parishes. This rightly emphasizes the centrality of sacramental worship and takes us back, as does much of the ASB, to the early Church.

As distinct from the sedentary office of Morning Prayer which, in company with Evening Prayer, derived from a conglomeration of material in the monastic offices, the Eucharist is a re-enactment of the greatest drama of all time and, moreover, involves the whole worshipping body present in a corporate way impossible in Morning Prayer. The Eucharist has physical movement, not only of the clergy and laity taking part, but through its construction and shaping towards a central point in the unfolding of that drama.

This applies especially to children, who invariably find Morning Prayer very static by contrast, which it is. On the rare occasions when my young family were taken to Morning Prayer they always complained, 'It's so dull and boring; nothing happens'.

The Eucharist provides a commitment, a personal involvement and a sense of community which is more revealed in Rite A, and to a certain extent in Rite B, than was ever possible in the priestly monopoly which under-

7

lines its counterpart in the BCP. The concept of the family gathering together around the table has been taken up and discussed in many commentaries. It has understandably been carried further through Rites A and B in terms of involvement and togetherness, though, as we shall later see, this can present problems for the music. Involvement can spill over into a chummy and matey type of worship with, *in extremis*, that extra spoonful of sugar which suggests, sometimes arrogantly, that a traditional choir, especially a robed one using choir stalls, is out of place and even possibly an embarrassment or deterrent.

(b) Evening Services
With the demise in many instances of Morning Prayer and the resulting move towards eucharistic worship, has come the putting of all the eggs into one basket. We tend now to worship as a family relatively early in the morning, which leaves the rest of Sunday free for an ever increasing variety of leisure pursuits. This is fair enough and seems to have plenty of logic in it.

Sunday evening television, some of it broadly religious, has undoubtedly contributed further towards the change in the pattern of Sunday churchgoing, even in some instances to its decline. It has always been claimed that the Evensong graph started its downward trend when the BBC televised *The Forsyte Saga* on Sunday evenings, but the questionnaire sent to RSCM churches in May 1982 somewhat surprisingly revealed that sixty-one per cent of choirs still sing Evensong each Sunday.

FOOD FOR THOUGHT?
1. However much some would like to persuade us otherwise, it is undeniable that, by and large, in England we still have too many churches, too many services – and certainly too many hymns. I well remember my Dean at Exeter suggesting that the choristers go out before the Evensong sermon on a Sunday, saying that three sermons

in one day were more than any Christian should be expected either to endure or digest.

2. As worship ideally comes from the heart, so is the need for prayer to emerge as a contributory result of the music no less applicable today than at any other time, probably more so. The Church has always leaned heavily on music as an aid to its worship in much the same way as secular society has relied on and used music to express varying emotions. Song is innate in all of us and certainly no less in church than elsewhere. Perhaps, to quote Bishop Michael Baughen, we should 'let the music take the word off the page'.

3. The pattern of churchgoing which has now generally emerged is one which has come about through a combination of liturgical awareness and social patterns.

OUR NEW FOUND FREEDOM

The new services provide a greater measure of freedom than before in our worship patterns, and this applies no less to the music than to the spoken parts. How this is worked out will be a matter for each and every parish to determine as it thinks fit; but it must be through democratic processes of consultation, in the course of which there will probably be much heart searching, not least in matters musical.

Considerable experimentation will probably be needed, which means variation and alteration before a satisfactory pattern emerges which is acceptable to the majority. Experiment will sometimes result in rejection. We sometimes forget that one of the objects of experiment is precisely this and, moreover, this is the purpose of the exercise. While we now have an element of flexibility which we never knew before, this, with the accompanying opportunities and challenges it brings in its wake, can result in tensions and frictions. To overthrow tradition, especially in terms of music, may sound an attractive and trendy proposition to some, but it will seldom, if ever, provide a lasting solution acceptable to all concerned. Would that it were all so simple.

What we have constantly to remember is that there is now a part for *all* to play in the jigsaw puzzle of worship. In this, no one aspect must be either side-tracked or given undue prominence at the expense of others.

This togetherness or involvement sometimes proves hard to achieve so that all legitimate needs and interests are provided for. For example, in the BCP Holy Communion service, priest and choir in Anglo-Catholic churches have frequently assumed more prominence than the congregation, much of whose role in such circumstances has by tradition been fairly passive. Today, in such instances, even though the BCP may still be in use, there is a move towards involving the congregation more actively, though this is not always proving easy to realize and can all too readily run into difficulties through trying to fit square pegs into round holes.

Other problems, though for different reasons, can be encountered in ASB services, when the concept of involvement gets out of hand and everybody is more or less encouraged, and expected, to be doing everything *all the time*. This, as we shall see later, can result in legitimate problems for the musicians and the music. Is it a case of either/or?

THE CHARISMATIC QUESTION

In a not unrelated way we need to consider the musical implications of the Charismatic Movement. But firstly, is the concept of renewal so new or novel? Has the Holy Spirit necessarily been dormant or little in evidence during the past two thousand years? Why has so much so suddenly happened? Many would agree that the revealing of the Holy Spirit is in fact a continuing process as much today as in the past. Renewal implies discovery. The only difference is that certain groups within the

Church are today laying more emphasis on pentecostal worship – and attracting considerable publicity in the process. Fair enough, but less than fair when it is accompanied by an arrogance which not only threatens the traditional choir and music but sees it as an obstacle to certain aspirations.

If those responsible truthfully subscribe to the belief that all of us have gifts to offer, then surely through the process of current renewal in service patterns there is a place for all. Does renewal imply the need to abandon traditional music and musicians or to lower standards? Should it not rather encourage a degree of rethinking which for many of us would be no bad thing. Even so, spontaneous and improvised 'singing in the spirit', which is one of the hallmarks of charismatic music, is perhaps hard to take both because it is so recent an innovation and also because of its marked contrast to what many of us are geared to through our musical upbringing. Even so, the spontaneous has a precedent in the witness of the early Church.

I frequently hear it said 'Our church has experienced renewal and therefore we have moved away from a traditional choir and music'. Why 'therefore'? While we are agreed that the Church has, through the centuries, experienced renewal in one form or another, it has not *per se* jettisoned its existing music as part of the exercise. There is no one single place for one type of music, be it traditional or otherwise. Surely, and ideally, there could, and must, be a tolerance for *all* valid expressions of worship through the help of music.

In those churches where this has been thought through rationally (and I think of the Church of the Redeemer at Houston in the United States where seventeenth century Italian motets sung in Latin can be heard alongside choruses) it is clear that all shades of musical persuasion can coexist quite happily.

If churches are genuinely moving away from traditional forms of music and finding fulfilment in music more generally associated with charismatic worship, perhaps we need to explore the reasons for this. Could it be that the dullness, the lack of expertise and a stubborn resistance to change at all costs, which are factors only too evident in certain churches and their music, merely serve as so many nails in the coffin of traditional music?

For my own part, wherever I have encountered evangelical and charismatic music, I have seldom failed to be impressed by the amount of preparation and rehearsal which has taken place and the high standard of performance which has resulted.

THE BASIS OF MUSICAL CHANGE

Whereas before the advent of the ASB there was, broadly speaking, one main stream of music identified generally through the SATB choir, the use of Anglican pointing for psalms and canticles, with Merbecke, Martin Shaw's Folk Mass and a handful of other settings, we have now moved towards three distinct musical prongs, which are quite different from one another:

1. the traditional parish church choir using music according to its musical resources;
2. that which springs from the influence of Holy Communion Rite A;
3. folk music and 'pop', often with instrumental and choral groups 'leading' an informal type of worship.

The first we should expect to find well rehearsed and competent, while the second will be simpler in its concept and in its need for musical resources. The third will, by marked contrast to the other two, be far more spontaneous and sometimes, though by no means always, unrehearsed.

This book sets out to review the current situation and to offer constructive and helpful suggestions. It is not only the musicians who are bewildered by the course of events. I find that many of the clergy, congregations and choirs I come into contact with are equally bemused, though this does not preclude their genuinely wanting to do the right thing for their parish. The real problem lies in their not knowing how to go about it or how to work it out. In some situations the clergy seem as reluctant to seek help as are some of the musicians unwilling to be in any way deflected from their chosen path. I would suggest that either attitude reveals an insecurity.

Above all else, this is intended to be a resource book, its aim being to help clergy, musicians and, not least, congregations, all in equal measure. We are all in this together and it must be a joint preoccupation.

I have tried to offer guidelines towards finding the right solution for each and every contingency. No two churches are alike in their needs, nor certainly in their resources. The latter to a certain extent determines both the former – and the formula.

Whatever else the ASB may be, it is not an updated version of the BCP. It must therefore be approached, not least musically, as something distinctly different.

In what follows, while I shall endeavour to highlight a number of matters, certain background considerations have to be taken into account. For instance, while the Anglican Church seems in some respects to be moving away from liturgical forms of worship towards freer and less structured types of services, the Free Churches are correspondingly becoming more liturgically minded.

In all that has happened there is always the danger of taking up the cudgels in placing too much emphasis on change for the sake of change. Yet, in all the deliberations, planning, and the subsequent follow through to the publication of the ASB, too little has been said about the musical issues except in those areas such as the RSCM and other bodies with church music interests where one would expect to find comment. If there has been musical notice in a wider context, it has often been in the direction of publications such as *Hymns for Today's*

Church which, by dint of its shock-tactics approach, attracted far more press coverage than other publications or happenings more nearly focussed towards the mainstream of contemporary thinking.

Another pointer should surely be that while good music enriches worship, why do we sometimes seem to want to offload this in favour of music which is less than worthy and more likely than not to be impermanent?

A final thought on this subject is that certain aspects of the Oxford Movement, however valid they may have been 150 years ago, now need some rethinking in order to accommodate new approaches to worship. I refer especially to the moving of the focal point of action away from chancel and sanctuary and into the body of the church. All change, especially if it is within the usually conservative framework of the Anglican Church, needs to be very carefully thought out.

Succeeding chapters will deal with the liturgical changes, with the parson/organist relationship and with the music itself. Each is dependent and reliant on the other. Worship and, for that matter, music, have never been static and certainly cannot be today. We shall never get our liturgy completely right because it can never be fully perfect. It is perhaps as Dr Ronald Jasper put it when, as Chairman of the Liturgical Commission, he neatly suggested that 'liturgy is a dialogue between a perfect God and imperfect man'.

2

WHAT ARE THE CHANGES – AND WHY?

THE HISTORICAL BACKGROUND

In order to set the scene in the right perspective, we must first briefly trace the sequence of events which through three centuries have led to *The Alternative Service Book 1980*.

The Book of Common Prayer is a convenient point of departure because this has always been the 'official' prayer book since 1662. It resulted from its predecessor of 1549, where the emphasis was on edification through the use of the Bible and the daily offices, but with Holy Communion as the central act of public worship.

Give or take a little, this was the situation for nearly two centuries. Then the 1851 Church census revealed that Britain was by no means a churchgoing nation. The results, not least the evidence that out of the population of 18 million only about one-third ever went to church, led the authorities to ask questions, not only on what was wrong, but also on how to seek remedies. So it was that from 1858 onwards concessions such as Sunday evening services began to gain ground. With this, choirs and the singing of hymns became the norm and it is interesting to reflect that the first edition of *Hymns Ancient and Modern* appeared in 1861. From then onwards emerged in their fullest sense 'corporate acts of worship'.

From these and other happenings arose the first conscious moves towards revising the Book of Common Prayer. In 1904, the Royal Commission on Ecclesiastical

Discipline concluded that 'the law of public worship is too narrow for the life of the present generation.'

A quarter of a century later the proposed Prayer Book of 1928 was published. This in its turn led to the Alternative Services Measure in 1966 and the Worship and Doctrine Measure of 1973 which allowed the Church of England freedom to revise its services at any time and, more importantly, with the break from parliamentary permission which had hitherto been binding.

It is interesting to note that the ASB in fact contains many of the principles of the rival Puritan and Laudian parties which confronted each other at the time of the 1662 Prayer Book. It has, moreover, gone well beyond all that was envisaged in what, in seventeenth century language, was termed 'comprehension'. So, in many respects, the wheel has turned full circle.

As corporate worship is now the basis of Sunday churchgoing, with an emphasis on Sunday because the average lay person does not normally go to church on weekdays, it is hardly surprising that the Eucharist has gained in prominence. This means that in many instances the daily round of Morning and Evening Prayer is confined to cathedrals and religious communities. Around these services there is a corpus of music incomparable anywhere in the world. This is something of profound value, especially to visitors from overseas, even if we in Britain tend to take our cathedrals and their music for granted and as a matter of course.

Worship cannot be static any more than the music we use.

This then is the nub of the situation; and the reason for this book is the liturgical explosion which over the past three decades has affected us all in some way or another. If we in the Anglican Church look on this as a traumatic experience, think of the Roman Catholics who have thrown out the baby, the bath water, the bath and everything in the huge liturgical upheaval resulting from Vatican 2. This, by comparison, makes the Anglican reordering of services seem a very lukewarm affair. We must also bear in mind that whereas the Church of England exchanged Latin for the vernacular at the time of the Reformation, the Catholics took another four hundred years to do so.

THE THREE MAIN ASPECTS OF CHANGE

1. *The language of worship*

Whether it be in church or in the secular world, language is the one main means of communication we have with one another. It is certainly our sole means of verbal contact. There is always the danger, as we know only too well, that because we have by and large opted to update our ecclesiastical language – and personally I have no doubts about the rightness of this – all the ensuing arguments are often made to hinge on the mode of language rather than the objective of those words we use. What really matters is how we elect to use words as a vehicle for corporate worship.

Those who fight tooth and nail for the retention of Cranmer are perhaps fighting for the word, but in doing so they ignore other matters. As words must be the vehicle for worship so must such language be couched in set forms which will be intelligible and fulfilling to those who hear them.

In some instances the zeal for linguistic preservation has been carried to such an extreme that it has become something of a fetish which takes little or no account of such factors, though it will very quickly put up smoke screens to justify its activities. 'The letter killeth, but the spirit giveth life'.

Perhaps even more to the point is the renewing effect the new services have had. Writing to *The Times* a couple of years ago, Bishop Frank West said:

'. . . My own widespread and concentrated experience of parochial worship in the south west of England has convinced me that it is those congregations that have

17

taken the new services into their system which are showing signs of life and that those who are resolutely refusing anything to do with the new services are in decline or at any rate in a state of stagnation.'

To say that the ASB debases what we had before is a blinkered and shortsighted viewpoint which comes perilously close to retaining archaism for its own sake. It might perhaps be suggested that neither ASB nor BCP is the *only* form of life. It is all too easy for us to chase straws in the wind and to get our thinking out of perspective instead of getting down to basics – and realities.

While many of us would concede that the language of Cranmer is exceedingly beautiful, that it flows and has dignity, there are many others who find it a difficult vehicle for their personal worship, and they do so in the light of having experienced the ASB, not in default of it. To such people, the BCP seems a mass of verbiage, with the Holy Communion service lacking the structure which the ASB has restored. While there are some who would take the opposite stand, I would suggest that, whichever side of the fence we opt for, all of us might perhaps be more ready to accept that there is another viewpoint and that there is an urgent need for less condemnation and more tolerance towards the other point of view.

The Church of England has always been wide-ranging in its different approaches to worship. Many of us believe this to be one of its glories, as compared with the rigidity of the Roman Catholic approach. Let us then disagree, but without being disagreeable.

Finally, while on the subject of words, I would suggest that all of us, whether clergy or laity, should always have in mind that what we say in church can be made to sound intolerably dull and lifeless. This applies whether it be 1662 or the ASB. The Church of England sometimes has an uncanny knack of producing verbal monotony when it comes to proclaiming the good news of the Gospels. The remedy for this is not to go overboard and interpret words in such a way as to make them bizarre, but to conduct services with an awareness of the dignity of language with a spaciousness which allows a natural sequence of events to unfold without either rush or an unduly pedantic approach. It is not, as one clergyman suggested to me, 'As long as everything is loud and fast, God is duly honoured'!

In many respects, beauty of language speaks for itself and in church can be dignified and meaningful without resorting to the parsonic, a shortcoming to which the clergy can be particularly vulnerable.

2. *The function and role of music*

To move a stage further, we have in all this to remember that the music arises out of, and from, the words, not *vice versa*. We therefore have to continually bear in mind that in an ideal situation music is a vehicle for enriching in a new dimension words which otherwise would have been spoken. It is one thing to say 'Holy, holy, holy Lord . . .' but an entirely different matter to clothe those words in music, however simple or elaborate the musical resources and traditions of a particular church may be. This is true of every aspect of song, be it the operas of Mozart, the songs of Schubert, Bach's Mass in B minor, Elgar's *The Dream of Gerontius, Oklahoma!* or the operas of Gilbert and Sullivan.

Music in worship is the handmaid of worship and never an end in itself. It is one of the gifts upon the altar. Choirs, aided and abetted by their choir directors, have sometimes made the mistake of viewing music as a substitute for worship and encouraged others to make music a private and personal empire by using the church as a convenient and totally unrelated platform for their efforts.

3. *Our involvement in worship*

Our new services are designed so that a heavier emphasis than before is laid on *all* being actively involved. This may seem to be stating the obvious but it is the stuff of which ideal worship is made. Not least in this is the part which music should play. In the process we have experienced something of a turnabout in the traditional roles of clergy and congregation, with the latter having a new found freedom which in its turn demands a greater responsibility. Because we have greater work to do, more preparation is consequently needed if we are to participate more fully.

For those accustomed to playing a much more passive role in worship, this has come as something of a shock and perhaps in some measure accounts for the ironic fact that the quest for togetherness and involvement has sometimes resulted in the very opposite. 'We come at 8 o'clock on Sundays because we like the *old* service,' is a case in point. In a not unconnected way, whereas in the past the celebrant celebrated, it is now the president who presides over all, and that includes the music.

In an ideal situation, there will be a place as before for those who wish to worship through the music being an independent, though integral, part of the whole. We must make no mistake as to the continued relevance of silent worship, though it is sometimes questionable whether we are helped by our clergy as we should be to learn the process of praying through music and to use it to the full as part of the total concept of worship. Sometimes the anthem is merely a cosy interlude, casually slipped into the service to give the choir something to do on their own.

This emphasis on involvement in worship, which is very much at the heart of the new liturgical thinking, can be experienced at its most fulfilling in the service of Holy Communion which, in a unique and special way, gathers up and uses the whole people of God in the unfolding of a great drama.

This is perhaps best illustrated by a comparison between Holy Communion in the BCP and Rite A in the

ASB. In the former, the role of the celebrant is to all intents and purposes that of a monopoly, everything centering on the priest and, to a lesser degree, any others in the sanctuary. The priest takes the lion's share in the service while the congregation, apart from being involved in the Gloria, Creed, Sanctus and Lord's Prayer, have, for the most part, to be content with saying Amen at the end of long prayers. The priest quite pointedly tells the faithful to make *their* confession 'meekly kneeling upon *your* knees'. In the subsequent light of ASB services this makes the distinction between sanctuary and nave the more obvious.

By marked contrast, in Holy Communion Rite A *all* are more or less continuously caught up in a corporate involvement and, arising from this, a corporate responsibility. Prayers in the plural are now said by all and not solely by the clergy on our behalf. The laity are frequently asked to read the Epistle and sometimes the Gospel. They are often responsible for the intercessions, for bringing the elements to the altar as part of the offertory procession, and sometimes for administering the chalice. The passing of the Peace is a further way of bringing together clergy and congregation. Our greeting each other in this way and at this particular juncture in the service is a perfectly rational process, provided it does not get out of hand with the resulting congestion almost approaching Piccadilly Circus in the rush hour.

At its best, the ideal concept of liturgy can be likened to a jigsaw puzzle in which all the pieces must be present and must correctly interlock in order to produce the complete picture. Omit or lose one piece and the picture is incomplete. No one piece, moreover, is more important than another, for the one depends on the other. So it is with the liturgy.

Some would argue, and with some justification, that we have gone from the one extreme to the other and that the shorter prayers and the continual flurry of activity have resulted in a restlessness – some would say fragmentation. To this is sometimes added the virtual obsession that, at all costs, we must be finished and out of church in as short a time as possible, almost as if there were virtue itself in this.

We can so easily get our sums wrong by being additionally encouraged to believe that the corporate nature of worship demands that everyone is doing everything all the time, an interpretation of involvement which, if carried to its ultimate, would border on the bizarre. Our genuine and well motivated yearning for more togetherness must, nevertheless, take into account that parts of the service will be the prerogative of the parson while other parts will be that of the choir and congregation, either together or separately. Certain aspects of worship cannot by their very nature be corporate, for example anthems and motets sung by the choir or, for that matter, the sermon.

Leading on from this we need to consider the rationale of the thinking in some areas that a choir as such is an intrusion which detracts from worship, instead of contributing towards its completeness. I would go further and say that I believe many of the current problems we frequently hear about or actually encounter, and which involve the rival claims of the music, the musicians, the clergy, and that painfully overworked and misunderstood concept of 'congregational participation', stem from this one single factor, namely our failure to work out what inevitably must be something of a balancing act. The frightening conclusion is that the music, instead of fulfilling its role of helping to enrich worship, becomes a cause for divisiveness, even bitterness or resentment, among those who make up the sum total of the worshipping body. Have we sometimes as a result fallen short of grasping to the full our being the true body of Christ? There is much food for thought here, not least for the musicians.

4. *The geography of worship*

How we use our churches to the best advantage is something which must inevitably claim our attention as part of contemporary liturgical thinking and planning. So often we have to wrestle with the building and the restrictions imposed on it by immovable furniture.

One of the 'geographical' results of the Oxford Movement in the mid-nineteenth century was to make the chancel and sanctuary the focal point of visual activity for a congregation seated in the nave. The ground plan of many Anglican churches is familiar to all of us, the more so because many cruciform churches are identical in the way the furnishings are laid out. The element of predictability is all too familiar in church after church.

As part of the Oxford Movement thinking the altar was placed hard against the east wall, while the organ was more often than not sited in a small chamber in the chancel which afforded it little chance to speak out into the nave. To complete the picture, the choir, who had probably been housed together with an orchestra in a west-end gallery, such as the Mellstock choir immortalized by Thomas Hardy, were now moved into the chancel where, instead of singing to the congregation, they were split into two groups which sang across to each other. This antiphonal deployment of voices is almost as old as the Church itself and much church music has been written, and continues to be written, with this plan in mind. Whereas in a cathedral this works admirably, if only because the congregation in the quire sit around the choir, the confined space of most parish church chancels makes this impossible. Clergy, together with any servers or others helping in the service, contribute to the over-population of the chancel. A further factor is the traditional siting of the choir midway between altar and congregation which, rightly or wrongly, is considered by some to be a distraction for those in the pews.

In many instances a screen, which in medieval times

may have fulfilled a function long since dispensed with, provided the final barrier in effectively cutting off the chancel population from the congregation seated in the body of the church and often at some distance from the chancel. Add to this the reluctance of most congregations to sit in the front rows of seats and you have all the ingredients for the classic 'we and they' situation, which is entirely contrary to the geography of worship when services such as Holy Communion Rites A and B are in use.

Because much of the furniture in most churches is firmly secured to the floor, a solution to this problem is not easy to find, except with respect to the altar, which, if not a stone one, can be relatively easily moved away from the chancel and into the body of the church. In order to give more room for manoeuvrability the front two or three rows of pews may perhaps be removed. The problem then arises of what to do with the choir who, if they are to remain in the chancel, become more than ever remote from the congregation. It may seem logical to suggest that they face the congregation but it is very hard for a choir to function properly standing in long rows and with each member singing into the back of the person in front.

Where then do we position the choir? This problem has faced many a PCC attempting to come to terms with reordering their church to accommodate the new services. Nevertheless, a solution has to be found.

To suggest that the choir be put into any convenient space, either in the body of the church or at the west end, will not in itself suffice any more than putting the choir in among the congregation. For this, however well motivated, merely serves to make them lose their identity and probably become disgruntled in the process. Moves such as these are easy ways out and only contribute towards making a choir feel themselves to be second class citizens. The ideal choir, motivated aright, will consider themselves to be part of the worshipping body of the church and as such should not be off-loaded, as they sometimes are, in a casual way.

Against a background of more or less fixed furniture there must of necessity be a degree of experimentation, with the right either to reject or to try something else if, after a reasonable trial period, a scheme proves to be unacceptable. As far as is possible, flexibility should prevail, with the observations of all concerned taken into account. Not least in this joint consultation should be the views of the congregation who, after all, are on the receiving end and therefore probably have the most to gain or lose.

In an ideal situation, as in a modern church where much or all of the furniture may probably be mobile, it is a relatively easy matter to experiment. The best answer, where practicable, is to worship in the round. This allows everyone to see everyone else and to be fully involved. Seated in serried ranks may, for entirely different reasons, be acceptable in the theatre, but is a lot less satisfactory in a church situation.

During my time as organist of Exeter Cathedral we were able to dispense with cumbersome and ugly Victorian choir stalls in the nave. What replaced them, including the Bishop's throne and clergy seats, was fully and easily mobile. This allowed for the flexibility needed in a busy and much used cathedral in the twentieth century, not least in terms of concerts. One of the plans we adopted as ideal both for choir and congregation was

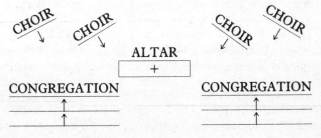

This permitted the sound of the choir to carry far more effectively into the body of the nave than when the two sides directly faced each other, and most of the sound was consequently deflected into the transepts.

It is perhaps significant to reflect that, whereas a century ago we moved the 'performers' together with the furniture they needed into the chancel, so now we are advocating and adopting the reverse process of bringing them back again into the body of the church. The reasons for this are sound enough even if not always easy to implement.

CONCLUSIONS

The geography of worship is a crucial aspect of the contemporary scene. This in its turn leads on to the visual aspect, something now readily accepted as a powerful ingredient of eucharistic worship. Choreography assumes a far greater significance in the context of the ASB than it does where BCP services are concerned. Perhaps one of the greatest mistakes we are liable to make is that of confusing these issues, for, as we have just seen, many of our Anglican churches are BCP furnished and BCP orientated. Once again it is a square peg and round hole situation, with the music and the musicians as much an issue as any other part of this particular jigsaw puzzle.

The changes we have experienced in the past thirty years inevitably affect the musical issues, in the types of music we use and how we equate the rightful claims of the musicians with those of the clergy and congregation. These, and other considerations arising from this, are matters likely at some time or another to affect most, if not all, of us.

3

THE MUSICAL CONSIDERATIONS

THE NEEDS OF TODAY AND THEIR PRACTICALITIES

We first need to remind ourselves that choral music in worship must, both in its choice and performance, fundamentally be the enrichment of an otherwise spoken text. This is its sole justification and if music detracts from worship, as sometimes can be the case, it does the very opposite by projecting a negative, even sometimes a destructive role. Moreover, in general terms, its function probably needs to be sometimes considered before its quality. I say this advisedly, bearing in mind that, because the church is a family, different types of music need to be explored as vehicles in the overall concept of worship.

In this context, it is not always a question of *either* traditional *or* more popular types of music. There is surely a place for both, sometimes even within the framework of a particular service. Both can be used and blended side by side, provided both are presented with integrity. What needs to be constantly emphasized is that 'folk' music implies a special idiom, to which the average church musician, trained in traditional music, cannot easily adapt, if at all. The two concepts are quite different and have to be treated as such.

In general terms, there is also a constant need for simple music, and with it getting away from SATB as being the unvarying yardstick of choral measurement.

For some unaccountable reason, choirs which cannot rise to SATB music tend to think of themselves as being second class.

I believe that in some instances churches opt for the more popular and quasi-secular types of music merely in default of not knowing what is otherwise available. A glance at RSCM publications will give some indication of what is currently in circulation in terms of 'music for the average choir'.

The need to set standards is paramount, the more so against the constant everyday background of the commercial, instant and repetitive nature of musak, which lacks that something underlining 'live' music which is necessarily relived each time it is performed.

The general position today is probably very little different from any other time in the past, except for its application in the light of a changing situation and the use in many instances of services relying fairly heavily on participation by all concerned.

Basic to this must be the need to safeguard the *rightful* place of music – no more and no less. This, in its turn, must take into account that in some churches music has by tradition played a more prominent role in worship than in others. Take, for example, the fruits of the Oxford Movement as they concern the music. These, though maybe valid enough a century ago, may now need some adjustment so as to be accommodated to the liturgical needs of our time.

We have to recognize that while in many evangelical churches music will often be slanted in the main towards hymns and perhaps choruses relying fairly heavily on congregational participation, there will be – if we must apply labels – Anglo-Catholic churches where choir music plays a much larger part in the scheme of things, and where the congregation is relatively, though not exclusively, silent.

In such instances there may be a rich array of musical

extras such as Propers, plainsong psalmody, office hymns and choir music. In such churches the ASB may not perhaps be in use. This element of comparatively silent worship, in which clergy and choir are responsible for much of the content of the service, is by design to help worshippers who probably wish for the most part to be silent participants or, at the most, to sing hymns and join in certain said parts.

In a similarly related way this underlines the sung daily Offices in our English cathedrals, though here the situation on Sundays has in many instances changed as the Eucharist, often Rite A or B, has increasingly become the norm, and with it a far greater degree of involvement by the congregation. Even so, apart from hymns and the said parts, the rest of the music will probably be sung by the choir, thus providing for those who do not necessarily wish to be involved as such, the freedom to participate silently while allowing the music to speak in its own right in enriching their worship.

The fact that many of our cathedrals have large Sunday morning congregations is evidence of a particular type of worship fulfilling a particular need. Those who may not subscribe to this approach should however respect its validity equally as much as those churches which place a heavy reliance on congregational participation.

These two poles, with all that ranges between them, display in a very real way the benevolent tolerance for all shades of persuasion and personal preference which is such a unique feature of Church of England worship. It emphasizes a freedom and flexibility denied to Roman Catholics and, although some would argue for or against this diversity, it is something which many would claim to be one of the glories of Anglicanism.

THE USE OF MUSIC
Whatever the situation and whatever the agreed proce-

dures may be, it is as bad for a choir to be under-employed as it is for a choir to be over used. The finding of a balance must take many things into account, not least these considerations, and that all concerned – musicians, clergy and laity – must try to arrive at a *modus vivendi* which relates to the needs of each particular situation. The fact that in many churches this has been worked out and implemented to the satisfaction of all concerned shows that agreed procedures can be found which are acceptable to all shades of opinion.

A potential danger is that in some instances where considerable choral resources, probably of a high standard, are available and in use, the music can assume such proportions as to overshadow the liturgy. This can turn into something of a take-over bid with the church becoming a convenient concert platform for the choir. When this happens, clergy and congregation have every reason to rebel. Once again the need has to be underlined for finding a balance between too much or too little music.

In a not unrelated way, it has to be emphasized that vocal music arises out of, and from, the words. This is no less real in church than in the field of secular music. In terms of the Church, this basic and fundamental truth must relate to what music in worship is all about, namely to clothe with music what otherwise would be said, while in the process providing an added and highly desirable new dimension which music uniquely offers.

THE CHALLENGE – HAVE WE ACCEPTED IT?
The sad reality is that English composers have not generally risen to the occasion by writing music for the new services. This, by comparison, is less true of other countries, least of all the United States, where the Liturgy Commission of the Episcopal Church has set about the task of meeting the need for new music in a way which makes the Church of England's efforts seem somewhat feeble and half hearted.

A partial reason for this perhaps lies in the subtle campaign mounted in certain quarters against the ASB texts. This has in its turn been given media encouragement, which has sometimes threatened to become a well orchestrated and almost hysterical propaganda campaign supported, as mentioned earlier, by those who view the subject with what many believe to be blinkered vision. It may be that the language of the ASB has faults in it and may lack something of the grandeur of Cranmer who, incidentally, was a genius who happened to be in the right place at the right moment. Furthermore, whereas the ASB dates in the main from 1980, it has to be borne in mind that the BCP has the patina and usage of three hundred years behind it, thus making it an exceedingly familiar vehicle for worship.

More to the point is the fact that we live in an age of immense opportunity for contemporary composers, a situation such as the Church has not experienced since the seventeenth century. All praise then to those composers, many of them amateurs in the accepted sense, who have risen to the occasion and have at least put pen to paper in a meaningful and positive way.

The ASB is a fact of life and a far more positive vehicle for setting to music than some of the third rate doggerel which we cheerfully accept without question as we plough our way through many a favourite hymn.

Here in the 1980s we have, as in so much of our worship, the age of immense opportunity to which I referred earlier. While the hymnody of our time has in many respects risen to the challenge of new words and new music, our new services have not as yet been generally served in the same way.

How, then, do we go about it – or how have we so far gone about it?

HYMNS

Hymnody is a basic ingredient of all types of worship within virtually every denomination. As such, it is everyman's music, a vehicle of popular piety, and an inescapable part of churchgoing. If it were for this reason alone and for none other, it behoves us to choose, sing and play hymns to the best of our ability. The fact that in some situations choir directors view hymns as a weekly chore or as a necessary evil to be dispensed with as swiftly as possible, is surely borne out by the routine and unadventurous way in which they are frequently sung and played and which does the cause of hymnody less than justice.

Although for most of us hymns are as evocative as smell, their choice is far too frequently approached in as perfunctory a manner as is their performance. 'We know what we like and we like what we know,' is for many the sole criterion beyond which they are not prepared to move one iota. Cyril Taylor has made the point that the tunes must be recognized as the senior partner, because for most people music generates more emotion than words.

How important it is then that the first hymn in a service is especially carefully chosen. We need something which will take us 'upward', such as 'Praise, my soul, the king of heaven', and not something merely 'horizontal' as, for example 'The church's one foundation'. Similarly, in Rite A Holy Communion the position of the final hymn needs to be carefully thought out. If it comes after the dismissal and not at some other place between the communion of the people and the final sentence, the whole impact of our going 'out into the world' is lost.

THE BACKGROUND TO HYMNODY TODAY

In order to understand fully the point at which we have arrived, we need to trace events over the past half century. In between the two world wars there was a limited, though significant, degree of activity mostly confined to a handful of fine new tunes which are now firmly established and widely used. Music by Vaughan Williams, Martin Shaw, Nicholson and John Ireland, together with some fine examples written for the public school scene, were an important part of what emerged.

The moves towards liturgical reform have contributed a parallel approach to hymnody, for the factors underlying much of the thinking behind our new services have also contributed towards a similar reassessment of hymnody.

The first significant move was in 1960 when the Twentieth Century Church Light Music Group emerged with Beaumont and Appleford as the key innovators. Although today we may view their work as reminiscent of the Noel Coward and Ivor Novello types of music of the 1930s, they should be given credit for setting in motion what was then a radical, and probably much needed, new thinking on hymnody. However much some of us may view such examples as transient and ephemeral – which is precisely what they were – the fact is that, to their credit, they retain a measure of their original popularity, not least in schools where they seem to answer a need. What they set in motion has now been generally overtaken by events and by successors such as Sydney Carter and Donald Swann, together with much of the contents of *The Sound of Living Waters*, *New Sounds*, *Hymn Praise* and *Psalm Praise*.

While it may be relatively easy to sing these hymns, the practicalities of playing them on the organ are a very different proposition. Written for the most part with the piano in mind, the accompaniment, especially for the left hand, frequently has to be adapted and rearranged for the organ. To play them on the organ as written is not only very difficult but does them less than justice. In many instances it is better whenever possible to opt for a piano and instrumental accompaniment, preferably played by those who are familiar with the idiom and know how to deal with it. The traditional church organist has, more than likely, been trained to play what is written, and therefore feels ill at ease when expected to adapt, and arrange, or even improvise an off-the-cuff accompaniment.

In *Songs of the Spirit*, published by the RSCM, Martin How has rewritten the accompaniments of ten of the more popular hymns, such as 'Amazing Grace', 'Morning has broken' and 'Sing Hosanna', so that they can be played more easily on the organ. Although we are currently engaged in our 'Reluctant Organist' scheme in converting pianists into organists, perhaps there is an equal need to convert organists into pianists.

In a similar way, the singing of these hymns, while natural enough to young people weaned on the popular music of today and the gyrations which invariably accompany it, is a very different proposition for an older generation conditioned to much more traditional types of hymnody and who, anyhow, probably have firm and somewhat inflexible views on what is appropriate or otherwise in church.

Whereas many American congregations have fewer inhibitions as to what they sing in church, we Anglo-Saxons, because of our longer and more conservative background, can easily become self-conscious, even embarrrassed, in such a situation. The moral here is not to attempt to force such hymnody on those congregations for whom this is more than likely to be anathema. To be told to 'get with it' and let your hair down cuts no ice with many people. It merely has the very opposite effect, for in many church situations you cannot cajole people in this way.

Ultimately, if you want traditional music you opt to worship at a church where this is the norm. If you want the opposite, then you transfer your allegiance accordingly. We must never make the mistake of forcing the issue. It seldom works.

The advent in 1969 of *100 Hymns for Today* was largely responsible for setting in motion the cult of the hymn supplement. The fact that many hymn books now have complementary collections of this nature is evidence not only of the enormous explosion in hymnody in recent years, but also bears out the need to make this additional material widely available. The fact of the matter is that so much of it is so good and has provided for a real need which was not being previously met. This is especially true of the words.

100 Hymns for Today includes a number of familiar tunes linked with new words, such as 22, 23, 46, 50, 79 and 80. *More Hymns for Today*, the second *Hymns Ancient and Modern* supplement, was published in 1981. It contains much of what emerged in the twelve years since the first supplement appeared and has especially highlighted the significant profusion of fine new texts which emphasize a positive theology and are relevant to the worship needs of today. This is in marked contrast to some of the sentimental jargon which, however nostalgically we may view it, underlines the shortcomings of much Victorian hymnody.

These texts are in marked contrast to some of the popular and heavily secular words which characterize some recent evangelical hymnody. These are probably far worse and more irrelevant than their Victorian forbears.

Other Anglican supplements, which include *English Praise* and *Hymns for Celebration* are further evidence of a policy which provides for specific needs. *English Praise*, which is *The English Hymnal* supplement, caters for a different type of congregation and need than *Hymns Ancient and Modern*.

The sum total is a dazzling array of new thought which has contributed immeasurably towards enriching the corpus of hymnody and has probably done so to a greater extent than in any other single era of church history.

It has also made us sit up and think about the hymns we use and why we use them. This in itself is no bad thing. Until a few years ago most of us took hymnody for granted, a fact further evidenced by the singularly narrow and frequently unadventurous choice which governed their usage. The Church of England has been notoriously lackadaisical over this as compared with the Free Churches. This is probably partially due to the fact that whereas in the Church of England the norm usually includes a choir which may provide anthems and settings of the canticles in addition to hymns, the Free Church approach depends heavily, sometimes exclusively, on a diet of hymnody as the basis of its music.

HOW TO DECIDE ON CHOOSING A NEW HYMN BOOK

As many parishes find themselves mesmerized by the multiplicity of hymn books and supplements now available, some pointers may be of help:

1. Opt for a book which reflects the general basis of churchmanship and thinking in your parish. If, for example, the church is fairly 'central' or traditional in its churchmanship, *Hymns Ancient and Modern* is more generally likely to be acceptable, and suitable, than *The Sound of Living Waters*.

Hymns Ancient and Modern New Standard was published in the spring of 1983. In addition to pruning down the contents of the 1950 edition to 333 hymns currently most in use, in many instances some of the tunes in keys too high for congregational use have been transposed down. Apart from this and the new edition having its notation in crotchets and quavers instead of white notes, the new book contains virtually no new material. It is merely an edition of convenience designed to be used alongside *Hymns Ancient and Modern Revised (1950)*. It is available with or without the two supplements of one hundred hymns.

* There is information on a number of hymn books on

pages 70 to 75 of the 1982 revised edition of my *Handbook of Parish Music* (Mowbray). Additionally, two of the Grove Worship Series booklets may be helpful. Robin Leaver's *A Hymn Book Survey 1962–1980* contains informative and comprehensive information on a wide variety of hymn books, while in *Hymns in Today's Language?* Christopher Idle deals in some depth with the texts of hymns, not least in the light of *Hymns for Today's Church*, the first book 'to be totally consistent in having its texts in a modern "you" form throughout'. Grove Books also publish *News of Hymnody*, a useful up to the minute quarterly leaflet.

2. A parish considering the introduction of a new hymn book should, before coming to a decision, have workshop sessions in which a number of books are studied and typical examples sung by the choir and/or congregation, or played by the organist.

3. While cost will obviously be a major factor, bear in mind that for most major hymn books (as with *The Parish Psalter*), an attractive introductory discount is usually available on orders made in bulk.

4. A supplement is a supplementary collection and is not intended to be used solely on its own, merely to reinforce and add to the contents of the parent book.

5. Before coming to a decision, bear in mind the various pros and cons. What you decide on will probably be binding for the parish for a number of years to come.

6. In the final analysis, even the best of new hymn books will be of little avail if the contents are played and sung with the dull monotony so often accorded to hymnody old or new.

7. We also need to remember that many traditional style hymn books are choked with chaff, with perhaps only a third of the contents being fully used. This was one of the reasons for the pruning of the Revised edition of *Hymns Ancient and Modern* where, even after thirty years, 300 of the 633 examples were found to be little used.

While this book is more concerned with resources than with performance methods, the practicalities nevertheless reflect certain points made more fully elsewhere, as for example in my *Making Church Music Work* (Mowbray) or *A Handbook of Parish Music* mentioned earlier. It may be of help to summarize, and emphasize some of the relevant points:

1. The need to relay the mood, character, and personality of a hymn. As each and every hymn has its own individuality, it follows that ideally no two hymns are alike.

2. The organ play-over, or introduction, is crucial in relaying what a hymn is all about. Not least in this is its tempo, which necessitates a strict pulse with no slowing down at the end, otherwise the process and objective of setting the tempo is destroyed.

3. While an uncompromising rhythmic vitality is of the essence in the singing and playing of hymns, the organist as leader is crucial to this.

4. Gaps between verses must be no less rhythmic, or consistent. All concerned must be given enough time to breathe, yet not so long as to threaten continuity.

5. The choice of stops can help the singers to assess the mood of a hymn. Not every hymn in a major key is necessarily loud and fast, any more than minor keys automatically suggest soft and slow.

6. Linked with this is the need for choir and organist to phrase, which means observing important commas. Similarly, one line of text which carries through to the next without a printed comma should be sung, and played, as one logical phrase.

7. Descants, either sung or played on the organ, can add to the impact of certain verses – and not always the last verse.

8. A free organ harmonization can also have the same effect, but only if the organist is something of an expert

in the matter. A re-harmonization which misfires is an embarrassment to all concerned. There are a number of books containing useful examples; these include *Organ Accompaniments for 24 Tunes from 'English Hymnal'*, *Accompaniments for Unison Hymn Singing* (RSCM) and *Last Verse in Unison*, a collection of twenty-four well known examples by Harrison Oxley. This is also published by the RSCM. Additionally, two books of 'Free Organ Accompaniments' by T. Tertius Noble, and comprising 150 examples in all, are published in the USA by Fischer.

9. When *Hymns Ancient and Modern* first appeared in 1861 it was by design intended more for the use of choirs than of congregations as such. Today, when a new emphasis attaches to the congregational singing of hymns, some of the existing keys, while maybe at a suitable pitch for an SATB choir, can be uncomfortably high for unison singing by a mixed voice congregation. The new (1983) edition of *Hymns Ancient and Modern* has, as mentioned earlier, most such examples in lower keys. There are, however, two sides to this particular coin, for although the congregation may now have hymns in suitable keys, where choirs are concerned the transposition downwards can make the parts too low for singing. This can apply especially to the altos. These matters need to be borne in mind when conflict arises on these rival claims.

WHO CHOOSES THE HYMNS?
As has been suggested elsewhere, there is much to be said for clergy and organist jointly choosing the hymns. This can help the one to understand better the work of the other and to emphasize further their joint responsibility in a very important part of their work. In short, it can be a case of two heads perhaps coming up with better results than one.

Nowadays, with so many avenues of choice, either in

the books themselves or in specially compiled check lists, there is no excuse for anything but a rational and wide ranging choice.

HOW MANY HYMNS SHOULD THERE BE IN A SERVICE?

One thing is certain, and that is that hymns should never be used as musical relief or to cover up what otherwise might be awkward silences. Alan Dunstan's admirable little book, *These are the Hymns* (SPCK), makes these and other points and is a book well worth consulting.

For most purposes, four hymns should be ample in any one service. This could be reduced to three if the choir sing an anthem or motet. Avoid at all costs the use of hymns as 'fillers' during the communion of the people. Two or three hymns used in this way is an abuse of the function and purpose of hymnody. How much better for the people to communicate in silence and *then* sing an appropriate hymn, or the choir an anthem.

In recent years there has been a reaction in some areas to structured worship, something the Anglican Church has in the past always heavily relied on as compared with the Free Churches. This wish for freedom finds a particular fulfilment in the Family Service which often has a calculated element of improvisation built in as part of its sequence of events. The danger is that such services can all too easily lack style, balance and a sense of development, resulting in a vague hotchpotch. A clerical feature of this type of service can all too easily be 'the spirit has moved me to put in another hymn'.

Worse still is the sudden changing of hymns during the actual course of a service. This can make a nonsense of the sequence of events and show a complete disregard, even courtesy, for the choir and organist who may well have gone to some lengths in preparing the hymns. Would that members of congregations who complain to each other about such frustrations said so to their clergy, for this is a matter which reflects little credit on a parson.

Nowadays, instrumental resources frequently exist in schools and elsewhere, and at a high level of ability. Do on occasion encourage these instrumentalists, either individually or in groups, to implement the use of the organ in church services. Hymns at the great festivals can be highlighted in an impressive and memorable way when so 'orchestrated'. The results of this can be heard in a number of churches, not least at All Souls, Langham Place, the church next door to Broadcasting House in London, where an orchestra is regularly used to good effect at Sunday evening services.

The use of instruments other than the organ, as will be seen later, can be extended to other areas such as anthems and voluntaries. Similarly, there is no reason why, in certain instances where suitable resources exist, guitars should not be used alongside more traditional orchestral instruments. There is no particular reason why these two types of instrument should necessarily be used in a pigeonholed polarity. Nor, in this context, should the use of the long playing gramophone record or cassette be ruled out. Given suitable equipment and the right choice of music, this can from time to time provide an effective contrast, for example, to the singing of hymns during the communion of the people.

PHOTOCOPYING

You may wish to use certain copyright hymns from a particular book or collection. Tempting though it may be to photocopy and hope that no one will find out, you may nevertheless be infringing the law and could be called to account by publishers, composers and authors, all of whom are very much on the alert today, and rightly so.

On the other hand, if you ask permission, you will find that in most instances publishers will be helpful and generous. If you are in any doubt – and copyright is a complex jungle – always find out first whether or not the material you wish to reproduce is copyright or not and, equally important, the conditions which apply. There are many ramifications and it is better to be safe rather than sorry.

INTRODUCING NEW HYMNS

There is an elementary psychology here. When a familiar hymn is announced and the organist plays over, without any prior warning, a new and probably unknown tune, he and tune will be assured of little less than a hostile reception. The fact of the matter is that most of us are innately conservative when it comes to what goes on in church services and, more often than not, we resent change. This is the more so, and understandably, when it is thrust on us without our being alerted in advance.

If, for example, a new tune is being contemplated for a hymn such as 'Abide with me', the way must be paved for so bold an innovation. The choir might introduce the tune by singing it as an anthem or, failing that, the organist might be asked to play it through a couple of times. In both instances this should be done during the course of a service. Having repeated this the following Sunday, the congregation will at last have some prior knowledge of what to expect. Whether or not they take to the new tune is another matter, but they will at least have had some warning and familiarization with what is about to take place. As a result, it could be that they are more likely to give the new tune a less biased hearing than if it is thrust on them unheralded.

THE MARRIAGE OF WORDS AND MUSIC

A further new look can be achieved, again through some sort of preliminary explanation, in the introduction of a hymn tune which, although perhaps generally associated with certain words, might find a new identity through partnership with a different text.

A number of examples spring to mind, such as the abandoning of the uneventful tune *Aurelia* to 'The Church's one foundation' in favour of *St Theodulph*, which is usually associated with 'All glory, laud and honour'. A further alternative is Vaughan Williams' majestic *Kings Lynn* (*English Hymnal* 562). Both tunes marry up so much more happily with the grandeur of the words.

Crediton (*English Hymnal* 206 and *More Hymns for Today* 169) fits like a glove to 'The Church of God a kingdom is', as compared with the tune *University* so often associated with these words.

The possibilities are endless, and it is not always necessarily a matter of different tunes being used as substitutes. Parry's *Rustington* (AMR 292 (i)) is an admirable alternative to the more familiar *Marching* which Martin Shaw wrote for 'Through the night of doubt and sorrow', while *Hyfrydol* (EH 301) with its long notes coinciding with the important words in the text, makes a most acceptable alternative to Stainer's somewhat superficial *Love Divine* associated with those words.

'At the name of Jesus' to Elgar's *Land of hope and glory* and 'O Holy City, seen of John' to *Auld Lang Syne* which, although they may at first seem somewhat strange, are two further examples where the marriage of unlikely music and words can produce interesting hybrids.

Many of us envisage a foreseeably long future for traditional style hymnody, providing we approach it in a visionary way, and do not necessarily always accept without question that because certain tunes and words have been badly married in the past this cannot be changed. By looking at the subject rationally we can surely find a new concept and meaning where it is needed.

If we persist with dull hymnody, of which there is much, and if the musicians sing and play traditional hymns in a monochrome and routine way, we cannot be surprised if our clergy, spurred on perhaps by a long-suffering congregation, decide to jettison the traditional in favour of folk, 'pop' or other types of trendy hymns. The fact that the last state may be worse than the first is neither here nor there.

SOME FINAL THOUGHTS ON THE SUBJECT

Hymns can be a profound and exciting part of worship, if only for the fact that everyone involved in the business of churchgoing is perforce confronted with hymns. As I mentioned earlier, while hymnody is an inescapable part of worship, by the very nature and construction of traditional hymn tunes, it can all too readily sound dull, monotonous and boringly repetitive. Musicians therefore have to extract every ounce of interest from words and music alike. Then – when hymns are performed in a visionary, rhythmic and vital way – the experience of worship takes on a new dimension.

It is strange that choir directors who can coax so much musical integrity from an anthem can have a blank spot where hymns are concerned. This applies no less to cathedral organists than to rank and file parish musicians.

If you want an exciting example of hymn singing as a guideline, listen to 'Hymns for All Seasons', a recording made by Sir David Willcocks and the choir of King's College, Cambridge, together with the Philip Jones Brass Ensemble. This gives some indication of what can be achieved, given variety, interest, vitality and, above all, some vision. It also discredits those who mistakenly believe that the one means to salvation, as far as hymns are concerned, is that they move quickly and loudly.

THE PSALMS

The Psalter has always been one of the unique features of Anglican worship. In their own special way the psalms speak of every conceivable facet of man's relationship to God. When allied to the Anglican chant and sung with a high degree of artistry, as in our English cathedrals, their various and changing moods sum up in a remarkably moving way a particular and much valued part of our Anglican heritage.

With the current emphasis on eucharistic worship and the resulting move away from Morning Prayer, we ran dangerously near allowing the psalms to become redundant, even if by default. The sharp decline in Evensong, choral or otherwise, was a further contributory factor, especially since Morning and Evening Prayer rely heavily on the inclusion of the psalms.

Our contemporary worship patterns therefore demand that we explore new ways in which to use the psalms. What has emerged is two-pronged, the one traditionally orientated and the other employing alternative methods, so that in musical terms they can be relatively easily performed, whatever the resources or situation.

THE USE OF THE PSALMS IN TRADITIONAL FORM

In cathedrals the psalms are said or sung daily as an integral part of Morning and Evening Prayer. In this way the entire Psalter is heard each month. For most of us churchgoing is restricted in the main to Sundays and, because many of the psalms are long and, as we shall see later, because their musical performance presents considerable problems, most churches have until recently been content to use a mere handful of well known examples such as 15, 23, 67, 121, 122, 130, 150 and sections of 119.

Recent thinking on the use of the psalms is reflected in the multiplicity of new lectionaries, both in Britain and throughout the Anglican communion. Whereas previously the choice proved to be mostly arbitrary, there is now no excuse, as even sections of a dozen or so verses from some of the longer psalms are appointed for use.

In this way we shall, over a period of time, become far more conversant with many more psalms. As we can now use them in relatively small chunks, there is less demand on the sometimes limited choral resources of a church.

PSALMS AT HOLY COMMUNION

While it would at first seem that there are few places where psalmody can be integrated into the Eucharist, there are in fact a number of strategic moments where the psalms can be used to good effect and in sharp contrast to hymnody. An element of flexibility and a little imagination can contribute in no small measure towards psalmody highlighting certain aspects or features of any particular service.

Where there is a choir, possible places for psalmody during Holy Communion are as follows:

1. THE GRADUAL. Eight or ten verses sung by the choir alone, with or without organ. In those churches where an Old Testament lesson precedes the Epistle, a psalm could link the two lessons, in which case a short hymn could be sung between the Epistle and the Gospel. It is important to ring the changes. In all such instances it is probably best for the congregation to sit and follow the words.

2. THE INTROIT. On certain occasions, such as the penitential seasons, a short palm might otherwise take the place of an opening hymn. It should be decided by consultation with all parties whether this should be sung by everyone or by the choir alone. Congregations have every reason and right to want to sing at the start of a service, and on most occasions should be encouraged to do so.

3. AT THE COMMUNION. Here a psalm can sometimes be sung by the choir as an alternative to a hymn or anthem.

4. AT THE END OF THE SERVICE. I often think back to my days at York Minster and the Sunday Eucharist. After the Blessing there would be an organ improvisation

which built up to a great climax leading into the choir singing Psalm 150 as an unaccompanied recessional. This was special to York Minster, and it was very good theatre as well, though I would not suggest this every Sunday in a parish situation. What I would suggest is that something like this might be done on occasions such as Easter Day but, as always, providing you have the necessary resources. In such a case, its rarity value would probably make it the more memorable.

In all instances such as the above or, for that matter, any other suitable occasions, it will greatly help if the reason why a particular portion of psalmody is being used is explained to the congregation.

Of no less relevance is the need for flexibility in determining the week by week routine. It is so easy to allow an uncompromising rigidity to determine any sequence of events.

What has been suggested also presupposes a proficient choir which can cope with psalms. There is little worse than an inadequate choir struggling with the complexities of psalmody.

THE CANTICLES

Some, such as Venite and Jubilate, are psalms in their own right. Others, including Te Deum, Benedictus, Benedicite, Magnificat and Nunc Dimittis, although not psalms in the accepted sense, have by long tradition been pointed for singing to Anglican chants. Of these, the seventh century Te Deum, being conceived in an entirely different mould from that of Hebrew poetry, is the least easy to accommodate within the framework of Anglican pointing. This accounts for the angularity which results from our trying to treat this fine poem of praise in this particular way with verse after verse spun out laboriously. Although Te Deum is frequently sung in this way, the result is less than edifying in verses such as 'Thou art the King of glory, O – O – O – O – Christ'.

47

The canticles are by their very nature an entirely different proposition from the psalms, whether they be the traditional texts or the new material found in ASB, of which there is a multiplicity for both Morning and Evening Prayer. Even so, there is the benefit of familiarity, as canticles, unlike psalms, are generally repeated every Sunday. This, in terms of the ASB, is further helped through their being available only in a pointed version, and one based on the familiar principles which underline *The Parish Psalter*. It is of immense value and consistency to have now one uniform, and official, version.

THE CHOICE OF A TRADITIONAL PSALTER

Assuming the BCP texts are used, *The Parish Psalter* is by far the best, and probably the most widely used. Based on a simple and consistent method and with the minimum of hieroglyphics, it is not only logical but also, because the natural inflexions of the words partner the music, it flows the more easily. Sydney Nicholson, its editor, exercised great care and forethought in the choice of the chants, especially for the canticles, where congregational involvement is likely to be at its greatest. The melodic line, often moving from note to note by step, is especially helpful to congregations. As with many hymn tunes (see page 39), some of the psalm chants have a tendency to be pitched in too high a key for congregational use. A compromise over the problems of key and a choice of chants acceptable to both choirs and congregations, is part of the *raison d'etre* of the RSCM Chant Book.

As with many of the major hymn books, there are attractive introductory grants in the shape of generous discounts for churches initially purchasing copies in bulk. Information on this can be obtained from the publishers, The Addington Press, RSCM, Addington Palace, Croydon, CR9 5AD.

As the official psalter linked with the ASB, this is only available in a uniformly pointed version. The language has been updated by a distinguished group of scholars headed by David Frost. As compared with the ASB services where the reshaping has been more drastic, the overall changes in the Psalter are surprisingly small and generally in detail only. The brief of the translators was that they produce a version which would sing easily. With this in mind, the committee worked in close liaison with those responsible for the pointing.

The great virtue of the pointed ASB Psalter is that it is the one and only official version. In this it contrasts favourably with the multiplicity of published pointed versions of the BCP psalm texts, which range from *The Cathedral Psalter*, where the editors put the cart before the horse in making the words fit the musical needs, to the galaxy of 'speech rhythm' versions which appeared in the 1930s, all purveying pet theories and ideals purporting to be *the* answer. The resulting confusion was increased by those who chose to alter the existing printed versions to suit their individual whims.

Those psalms in the ASB Psalter appointed for use with the lectionaries are now available with chants. These are published by Collins Liturgical Publications. In many instances, such as the canticles and the most frequently used psalms, the chants are more or less identical with those to be found in *The Parish Psalter*, the underlying policy throughout being once again that of simplicity.

OTHER WAYS OF SINGING THE PSALMS

1. The RESPONSORIAL METHOD has become increasingly popular, and with due cause, the general principle being that after every two or three verses sung by choir or soloist, the congregation sing a simple phrase which emphasizes the theme of the psalm. In this way the

musicians bear the brunt of the non-recurring and more difficult material, while the congregation are left with a short recurring refrain which is musically undemanding.

Joseph Gelineau, a Belgian Jesuit priest, was one of the first to popularize this method and, although his particular approach is probably more readily attractive on the continent than in England, he nevertheless pioneered a way for others to follow. Father Laurence Bevenot's *15 Psalms to honour the Holy Eucharist*, published by Chester, are constructed on similar lines, but have the advantage over Gelineau in being set out in a more easily readable way. Here, as in other instances where there is no choir, it is suggested that a soloist be used.

Other collections include *The Psalms for the Church Year*, a set of twelve books linked with the three year lectionary. An SATB refrain using sixteenth and seventeenth century German and Italian music, is sung after every three verses of simple congregational plainchant. These books are published in the USA by Concordia but are available in Britain. Geoffrey Boulton Smith's *Responsorial Psalm Book* (Collins), together with Dom Gregory Murray's simple but highly attractive contributions to *English Praise*, the supplement to *English Hymnal*, are further examples.

Colin Mawby has produced two books of *Ten Psalms* (The Grail). Although basically for choir use, a congregation could join in the refrains with relative ease after a little preparatory explanation and rehearsal. Arthur Wills has written *Three Psalms of Celebration* (RSCM) which are also specifically for choirs and, although perhaps rather more demanding, effectively capture the mood of the texts. Finally, there is another RSCM publication, *O Come let us sing*, devised by Allen Ferns. This demonstrates the wide variety of ways in which psalm texts can be treated.

2. PLAINSONG. It is unfortunate that in some churches the

mere mention of plainsong frightens many who immediately associate this either with the Roman Catholic Church (who incidentally more or less universally abandoned plainchant after Vatican 2), or with the Anglo-Catholic wing of the Church of England. Be that as it may, plainchant is nevertheless the Church's traditional folk music and, as such, goes back to the earliest days. Although some plainsong can be ornate and complicated to negotiate, the charming simplicity of plainsong psalmody with its small melodic range (which is why it is written on a four line stave), its being in unison and ideally needing no accompaniment, ought to combine to make it readily acceptable in those areas where the more demanding SATB Anglican chant is difficult to negotiate satisfactorily. Alas, this is not so, for choirs persist with the Anglican chant almost as a point of honour, and whatever the results.

By contrast, the utter simplicity and enchanting flow of plainchant, with its lovely inflexions and its melodic rise and fall, somehow combine to make it breathe an aura of worship as much today as in any previous generation. Due largely to the work and enthusiasm of Dr Mary Berry, plainchant is now being discovered by more and more people. Writing some time ago in *Catholic Christian*, she described churches where '(Gregorian) chant is being discovered with immense delight and astonishment by an eager and responsive new generation who are too young to have heard it in Church as a matter of course . . . It is also being discovered by large numbers of young people who are seeking (often unconsciously) true sources of spiritual nourishment and enlightenment, but who are not committed to a religious faith'.

3. METRICAL PSALMS. The problems surrounding the singing of the psalms in the traditional mould of Hebrew poetry, coupled with the attendant difficulties of accommodating differing verse lengths, has led over the years to the use in certain situations of various types of

hymnody in which the substance of the psalm texts has been recast in rhyming verse and to which a familiar hymn tune is linked.

Although some of the versions may not be the ultimate in poetic utterance, and while some of the rhyming is, to say the least, forced, such as

> 'No longer hosts encountering hosts
> Shall crowds of slain deplore;
> They hang the trumpet in the hall
> And study war no more'.

metrical psalms offer a compromise which has some practical value.

Most of us sing metrical psalms without realizing it. A glance at any hymn book will quickly reveal just how much of what we take for granted in hymnody is in fact metrical psalmody. 'Before Jehovah's awful throne' (Psalm 100), 'As pants the hart for cooling streams' (Psalm 42) and 'Pleasant are thy courts above' (Psalm 84) are but three random examples out of many.

4. ANTHEMS. Down through the centuries composers have always been attracted by the beauty of the psalms and have set them to music as anthems in their own right. The entire spectrum of utterance from penitence to praise, with all that lies between, has resulted in an enormous repertoire ranging from short and simple pieces to full scale anthems for cathedral use. The choice is legion and there is something for every conceivable situation and type of choir which can be easily linked to the theme of a particular Sunday or service.

5. SAID PSALMS. In any circumstances there is much to be said for sometimes saying the psalms – and doing so sitting rather than standing. Provided they are said in a natural voice and made to flow, they will take on a new and distinctive dimension. As with the singing of the psalms, an antiphonal approach is best, such as, for example

(a) alternate verses said by parson and people;

(b) those on one side of the church alternating with those on the other;

(c) male and female voices alternately.

Other variants can be devised, but in all instances a slight pause at the mid-verse colon is desirable, if only to emphasize this distinctive feature of Hebrew poetry. It is also probably best if complete verses, rather than half-verses, be said antiphonally.

It cannot be over-emphasized that in all situations it is far better, and certainly more edifying, to say the psalms well than to sing them badly.

Whatever ways may be decided on for using the psalms and canticles, there should always be flexibility in the way they are approached. If, for example, a Gradual psalm is to be used, consider ringing the changes between Anglican pointing, a responsorial version, a metrical psalm and a spoken example. This adds variety and helps a choir and congregation to be more aware of the meaning of a text.

Finally, I hope I may be allowed to mention my book *The Psalms – their Use and Performance Today*, which deals exhaustively with the subject and which is published by the RSCM.

SERVICE SETTINGS

HOLY COMMUNION

Before the advent of Series 2 (Rite B) there were, generally speaking, three distinct and contrasted customs in terms of BCP services:

1. Those churches where the services were said but with the inclusion of hymns, usually at the beginning, at the Offertory and at the end.

2. The parish church with average, or even less than average, musical possibilities. Here, in addition to hymns, perhaps Sursum Corda, Creed, Sanctus, Benedictus, Agnus Dei and Gloria, would be sung by both choir and congregation. Merbecke, Martin Shaw's 'Modal' Service,

Nicholson in C and Harris in F were some of the more popular settings then in vogue. Whatever their overall musical merits or otherwise, they were at least functional and proved particularly suitable to the needs of that time. 3. Major parish churches and cathedrals, where the same parts of the service would be sung but to more elaborate settings such as those by Stanford or Darke in F. As these were specifically choir settings, the congregation would be listeners or would participate silently.

HOLY COMMUNION RITE B (SERIES 2)
The textual changes here were so small and few in number that the choir either made the necessary small adjustments to existing settings or merely continued to sing what they had always done. The prefatory notes to the services allowed for this. A concession frequently introduced into parish services, and sometimes even cathedrals, was that of singing the Creed to Merbecke or perhaps *Missa de Angelis*. This not only involved the congregation at a focal point which many consider should not be exclusive to the choir, but also helped to restore a balance to the service by reducing the amount of music at this particular juncture, some of the extended choir settings of the Creed being considered unduly long. Even so, there is much to be said for the use of such settings from time to time as part of the ethos of a congregation worshipping silently. There is something magical about the final bars of the Creed of Stanford in B flat and Darke in F which capture the vision of the words in a way which Merbecke cannot, nor was probably ever intended to do.

HOLY COMMUNION RITE A (SERIES 3)
The advent of a modernized and, by comparison with Rite B, much altered text, provided a unique opportunity for composers. The fact that many composers have not risen to the challenge is another matter and one which

was debated earlier (pages 30 and 31).

The adapting of familiar settings, such as Merbecke, Martin Shaw and *Missa de Angelis*, to the new texts is a poor compromise of convenience which dodges the issue and only serves to confuse those long accustomed to the much better originals. After all, the composers wrote their music specifically for the 1662 text.

Because it was intended that in ASB all should take part, those composers putting pen to paper have invariably done so in an austere, sometimes even unadventurously pedantic, way and more often than not have written for unison voices. There are, however, exceptions such as John Rutter, who was first in the field, leading the way which others emulated.

It must be reiterated that because of the emphasis on involvement this simplicity in the music tends to minimize and, by implication, to play down the role of the choir. So much unison singing comes as bad news to many choirs. Furthermore, the situation regarding the Creed, to which is now added the Lord's Prayer, has moved a stage further than what was mentioned above, in that it is now almost universal for these to be said. This involvement of the whole worshipping body is, for obvious reasons, desirable at these particular points in the service.

Where more elaborate choral resources exist, there is much to be said for the option of retaining the traditional settings of the 1662 text. This ensures that a particularly significant contribution to the repertoire is kept in use and gives those choirs able to perform such music the opportunity to do so. Nor should we underestimate the value of this, given the right conditions.

In many instances, such settings are successfully integrated into Rite A and Rite B services without endangering in any way the corporate nature of worship. They merely provide a different emphasis. Even so, there are situations where it may be felt desirable to have

Rite A language throughout, whether it be said or sung. This is understandable, although it can restrict the musical possibilities.

As always, it is a question of musical expediency, together with the degree and extent to which any one particular aspect of a service is subjected.

Unlike the spoken parts of a service where the juxtaposition of seventeenth and twentieth century language seldom results in a happy compromise, no problem arises when one language is said and another sung. The exception to this is the commonly accepted practice nowadays when Collect, Epistle and Gospel in contemporary language versions are used in 1662 or Rite B Holy Communion services. This further applies to the singing of Latin masses which marry quite happily with Rite A language. Neither is incompatible with the other.

The RSCM publishes a list containing information on many of the available settings of Rite A Holy Communion, each with an explanatory note relating to any specific features or innovations. This list is updated at regular intervals. In the July 1982 issue (No 3) of *News of Hymnody* (Grove Books), Peter Harding produced a survey of Rite A settings. Both are useful check lists.

So far, no real successors have emerged to the settings of Martin Shaw, Merbecke and the like which were so universally used from the 1930s onwards until the advent of the new services. While churches tended to adopt one particular setting and use it week in and week out, nowadays there is in many instances a more flexible approach. Some churches elect to use two or three settings in rotation, or even to use parts of one service one week and different parts on another Sunday. In this way there is an element of variety which can, furthermore, make congregations and choirs think about the words through the music.

Looking back in hindsight, I am more and more convinced that musically we set off on the wrong foot where Holy Communion Rite A was concerned. Composers were encouraged to provide at one and the same time for *both* congregation and choir, and in that order. John Rutter's setting proudly proclaims on the title page that it is 'For congregation and choir' – and in that order. However well intentioned the motives, most settings have compromised to such an extent that in the event much of what has resulted has, I believe, failed to satisfy either choir or congregation. The two needs are widely differing and probably not by any means compatible. It has consequently proved difficult to satisfy choirs without providing music too demanding for congregations while, by the reverse token, choirs are frequently disgruntled at being confronted with music which fails to stretch them or their capabilities and which they consequently find unfulfilling. What has so far resulted is, in the main, neither the proverbial flesh nor fowl.

I suggest that we look at this situation afresh and that we do so with some urgency, and also that composers consider the approach sometimes adopted in the Roman Catholic Church where, interspersed with choir music as such comes an easy, memorable, and repeated refrain for the congregation. Something on these lines could conceivably cater for all abilities and generally prove more satisfactory, in much the same way as Gelineau and others writing responsorial psalmody have sought to find a solution to the difficulties inherent in singing the psalms.

Furthermore, in a climate of opinion where we glibly talk of the togetherness and involvement of all in contemporary worship, if the music is a divisive force we have little cause for complaint when parochial policy and decision making is at the expense of the musicians.

A question mark arising from this, and frequently aired, concerns what is seen as a possible dichotomy, in that having a liturgy in which all are intended to take part, what is the point of having what can be thought of as an élite, separatist, group called the choir? The situation can be further complicated by the choir playing its main role in those very parts of the service which are specifically orientated towards participation by the entire worshipping body. Provided the situation is fully accepted by all parties, the choir will fulfil its particular function as a group designated to lead the singing. In this way a balance can be maintained and with less risk of the choir making a take-over bid in Gloria, Sanctus, Benedictus and Agnus Dei.

The integration of a choir, whether as leaders of the music or to sing those parts of the service as a purely choir slot, can be a viable proposition provided there is give and take on both sides which will allow a measure of adapting to the specific needs and resources so often mentioned in these pages.

MORNING AND EVENING PRAYER

In most churches where there is Mattins, it is more than likely that this will be BCP, and that in addition to the normal quota of hymns and psalms the canticles will generally be sung to chants. Where the choral resources exist, settings of Te Deum and/or Jubilate and perhaps Benedictus may on certain occasions be included.

Evensong is frequently a mixture of BCP or ASB. A survey carried out in 1982 by the RSCM revealed that no fewer than sixty-nine per cent of those churches affiliated to the RSCM who completed the questionnaire sang at least one BCP Evensong monthly. Only sixteen per cent used ASB Evensong.

Although many churches will sing the Evensong canticles to chants, choral settings of Magnificat and Nunc Dimittis are on special occasions more likely to be encountered than their Morning Prayer counterparts.

In order to provide a sharing out of resources, if Magnificat is sung to a special choir setting, then Nunc Dimittis might be sung by all to a chant, or vice versa.

Alternatively, the use of metrical versions of these canticles, such as 'Tell out, my soul, the greatness of the Lord' (*100 Hymns for Today*, 89) and 'Faithful vigil ended' (*More Hymns for Today*, 120), provide variety and perhaps more readily tend to involve the congregation. If one canticle is sung to an Anglican chant, perhaps the other might be one of these hymn versions.

As yet there are relatively few settings of the ASB text of Magnificat and Nunc Dimittis. The RSCM publishes one by Jack Hawes, while Weinberger have come up with various examples by Alan Wilson. Although in general the prevailing situation with regard to whether or not choirs are allowed to sing settings of the Canticles will determine policy, we nevertheless now have a new situation which calls for new music. It is to be hoped that composers will produce suitable and relatively simple choir settings for parish use, not only of Magnificat and Nunc Dimittis but also of the other Canticles now included in ASB Evensong.

Until such time as our cathedrals more generally include ASB Evening Prayer, we are unlikely to find many settings of the evening canticles to parallel the enormous wealth of music which was triggered off three centuries ago by the appearance of the BCP and which has been continuously added to by each successive generation of composers.

OTHER ASB SERVICES

As far as these are concerned, the extent of the music will be dictated by the needs of any given situation. The Wedding Service is the one likely to be most widely used in terms of the music and, as a guide to this both for clergy and musicians, Kenneth Stevenson has produced for the RSCM *The Marriage Service with Music*.

For general hints on music and allied matters in the context of the ASB, Addington Press (RSCM/Mowbray) have published *Music and the Alternative Service Book*, a comprehensive little guide book covering all aspects of the subject.

For ASB Morning and Evening Prayer, the RSCM have published a setting by Andrew Fletcher together with an adaptation of the traditional ferial versions.

ANTHEMS
Here we have a veritable bonanza of material ranging from the very simple to the highly ornate.

It is perhaps significant that the Church has always attracted composers to an extent unknown in any other single branch of music. Incidentally, this includes some very fine examples written by those who were unbelievers or even agnostic. Whatever conclusions we may, or may not, draw from this, the fact remains that the words of the Liturgy, the Bible and the religious poetry of every generation have exerted a magnetism for composers matched only by what painters have contributed in a visual context towards a similar enrichment of the Church.

An interesting and comparatively unique feature in England has been the swing in our time away from the cathedral organist as composer towards those by no means necessarily associated primarily with the Church. Into this category come such names as Vaughan Williams, Britten, Howells, Walton, Leighton, Mathias and Rutter, whose combined output for the Church is as significant as it is sizeable, the more so when it is seen alongside their total output. Compare this with the last century when cathedral organists, and relatively few other composers, were writing church music in great profusion, surprisingly little has survived, and much of what has survived remains unused in many a choir vestry up and down the country. Today there may only be a mere handful of cathedral organist composers, but their sum total of music can be assessed alongside the mainstream of twentieth century composition.

Nor has the resulting music been confined to liturgical needs as is shown by the many 'concert' settings of the Mass, together with countless cantatas and oratorios. Verdi, who was *par excellence* an operatic composer, nevertheless wrote a Requiem which has been referred to as his best opera. Brahms was not essentially a composer of religious music yet his German Requiem is one of his finest works, and the same can be said of the 'church' music of many other composers, not least the B minor Mass of Bach.

Some of the best and most moving church music of any era has been the simplest in concept and demands. Woe to the choir director who views such gems as Tye's *O come, ye servants of the Lord* and Mozart's *Ave verum corpus* as simple and therefore inconsequential. These and countless other miniatures need more in artistry and performance than many a work known to be more technically demanding. In church music 'small is beautiful' as truly as in any other situation.

Many of us need to be visionary and generally far more wide-ranging in our choice of anthems and motets, always bearing in mind their power to reinforce and highlight a specific point in a service. We also need to consider giving a choir plenty to keep it occupied, with the anthem being as much a focus of special interest for them as for the congregation.

The needs of each church, at what point in a service an anthem should be sung, the appropriate length, and any other eventualities, should always be taken into account when determining the choice. As with hymns, it is suggested that anthems be chosen jointly by the organist and the parson, though with the casting vote in this instance being to the former. Given that the appropriate choice ensues, the anthem can be of immense value as an additional bonus to worship, the more so from the congregation's point of view if they are encouraged to see this, in company with the sermon, as an integral and prayerful part of a service and not as a diversion, however pleasant, from the main business of worship.

The anthem should never be a performance merely to show off the expertise of a choir.

SPECIFIC USES FOR ANTHEMS AND MOTETS

1. MORNING AND EVENING PRAYER. While the traditional place for the anthem in BCP services will generally be after the third collect, an introit at the start of a service and perhaps sung at the west end of the church or even in the vestry can be as useful a mood setter as it can be a means of pin-pointing the theme of the Sunday or festival. The same applies where the ASB is in use, though here a short choir piece could sometimes take the place of one of the canticles. The comparative rarity value of doing this can make it the more impressive and memorable.

2. HOLY COMMUNION. A short motet can be particularly effective as an introit, especially if sung in a different part of the church from where the choir sit.

Peter Aston and Richard Shephard have set some of the ASB Seasonal Sentences. These short starters of fifteen to twenty seconds each are published by the RSCM. They can effectively set the mood of a service, whether it be Rite A, Rite B or the BCP.

The Gradual is another obvious place for a short anthem, as is the longer time available during the communion of the people. If the choir communicate before the congregation and then move either to a side chapel or some other suitable part of the church away from the chancel, the sound can be impressive and will not distract either choir or congregation, as it might do when the people are moving through the chancel to the communion rail while the choir sing in the stalls.

The offertory is a further place where, on occasion, an

anthem might take the place of the customary hymn. Though not often encountered in England, certain parts of the Anglican communion have adopted this to advantage.

3. SPECIAL SERVICES. The opportunities here are wide ranging, with the anthem capable of playing a significant function as a musical centre piece. Given enough warning, a special one-off service can be the occasion for the choir learning a new anthem, which will not only highlight the occasion but subsequently become part of the repertoire.

In general terms, the need is for short, simple, all purpose material. Nowadays there is less resistance to Latin texts and, on all counts, it is far better to sing music in the language in which it was conceived, whether this be Latin, French, German or Italian. It is suggested, however, that an English translation be given to the congregation, either verbally or printed in the weekly bulletin.

The use of canticles as anthems in their own right adds a new opportunity for performing a wide variety of music in another, though no less relevant, context.

In terms of the composer, the multiplicity of opportunities is legion, not least in the challenge to provide for the resources available today in any given situation. Many choirs for one reason or another are depleted or are incomplete in voice parts, therefore music needs to be available for each and every situation. How much better to have music of integrity and usefulness for a unison group, a two-part choir (sopranos and basses) or, as so often transpires, a choir without tenors. The RSCM has, among other publishers, set out in recent years to provide for such contingencies and, within these circumstances, to meet a very real need through a flexible approach.

What is needed today is far less persistence in perpetuating a heavily chordal and sometimes indigestibly uneventful SATB style. A mere glance at much nineteenth century church music – and a not inconsiderable amount of twentieth century writing – reveals an almost monotonous dullness which frequently lacks vision and certainly attractiveness as compared with much secular music of the period.

Why is it that the Church can have this stultifying and negative effect on some of those who write for it? The answer may partly lie in the fact that in church music there is a high incidence of amateur organists setting pen to paper and doing so with little of the technical skill or expertise needed. A readymade platform for inflicting the results on a congregation, and the fact that composers are often encouraged to do so by those around them, do not help matters.

The three basic ingredients of *all* music – a good melodic line, interesting harmonies and, above all perhaps, a rhythmic vitality – need to be applied no less to church music than to any other branch of composition. Not least in this is the fact that we live in an age extremely susceptible to rhythm. It is in precisely this area that the contemporary composers mentioned earlier who are not exclusively connected with the Church have brought a refreshingly new and much needed dimension and vision which have greatly enriched the current scene.

Finally, two further possibilities:

1. *Recitals and concerts*. A significant part of the present day situation is the increasing use of churches for recitals and concerts. The fusion of fine music with the visual environment, together with the sense of occasion which is seldom realized, nor possible, in the clinical surroundings of the concert hall, have done much to further this ancillary use of churches. Unrestricted in this instance by liturgical considerations, the possibilities are considerable.

2. *Repertoire*. Reliable check lists are hard to come by, if only because of the reluctance of publishers nowadays to issue catalogues and send out specimen copies. The fact

that so much material is currently out of print and likely to remain so is a further hazard.

The RSCM provides lists in specified categories but is equally hampered by these problems. Reviews and publishers' lists, however infrequent, and, not least, word of mouth information, are the only really reliable ways of keeping in touch with what is available.

THE USE OF INSTRUMENTS OTHER THAN THE ORGAN

There are considerable opportunities here before, after or during the course of a service. Whatever form this may take, it should always be viewed as alternative or additional to the normal use of the organ. In most circumstances it should not be opted for as a convenient substitute, however attractive this may at first seem, especially if you perhaps have an elderly organist set in his or her ways and whose playing may not be as inspiring as it might be. The prospect of a group of proficient young instrumentalists from a local school is a tempting proposition, assuming they can be persuaded as a group to play Sunday by Sunday. Against this you will have to weigh up the pros and cons of your organist who is probably doing the job conscientiously, if not perhaps excitingly, and maybe has given long and dedicated service to the church.

The organ has a particular quality of sound which readily seems to identify it, through association, with Christian worship. It has, after all, been used as such for a very long time and has qualities which make it eminently suitable for its task, though not exclusively so.

INSTRUMENTAL MUSIC DURING SERVICES

From time to time, especially on the great festivals and other important occasions, the addition of brass, wood-wind and percussion, can highlight a service in a significantly unique and memorable way. This applies especially to moments of climax in great hymns. Similarly, when two or three choirs combine forces, anthems such as Vaughan Williams' 'O clap your hands' or Finzi's 'God is gone up' take on a new dimension when orchestrated in this way, as will Bach's 'Jesu, joy of man's desiring' if the flowing tune in the accompaniment is played on a solo oboe accompanied by the organ.

While orchestral parts are available for some anthems, more often than not it is a question of someone with the necessary flair writing out the parts for hymns which might also include instrumental, as opposed to the more familiar vocal, descants. Vaughan Williams' Coronation version of The Old 100th (All people that on earth do dwell), is always a great favourite and can be obtained from Oxford University Press.

Finding the players should not be too difficult. Apart from people in the neighbourhood who may from time to time be willing to be involved, local schools can often be fruitful recruiting areas. The advantage here is in having a group from one school with the possibility of the director of music preparing the players in advance. Young people value the experience of playing in public, and to do so in a church can be a rewarding experience. Nor should the pastoral possibilities be overlooked, especially when families and friends of the performers may not be regular churchgoers or even churchgoers at all. In such a way, the congregation will value this new approach which also brings new insight into the music being presented.

Bearing in mind that composers in every generation have written church music scored for orchestra, it is surprising that we seem to place so much reliance on the almost exclusive use of the organ. Given that the resources exist and that a little imagination is exercised, the possibilities are enormous. These include the use of piano with organ and instruments used singly or in groups with or without organ and/or piano.

A further consideration is that certain modern hymns

such as those by Sydney Carter, Donald Swann and the 20th Century Light Church Music Group are mostly conceived in a pianistic vein and therefore sound best when accompanied on the piano. The carol arrangements of John Rutter are a further case in point, though these rely for their best effect on an orchestral accompaniment. As they are skilfully scored for a fairly large orchestra, the piano and organ may also be needed to fill in any missing parts.

WHEN THERE IS NO ORGAN. In certain circumstances there may be little reasonable expectation of finding an organist. In such situations, if the singing is not to be unaccompanied, some alternative form of support must be sought. The reasons why organists are not prepared to be committed on a regular week by week basis are many and various, some being legitimate and others excuses of convenience. Nevertheless, this is a fact of life, and there is no reasonable expectation of any significant improvement being likely in the foreseeable future.

As this type of situation is especially encountered in country areas, a single violin, flute, oboe or clarinet is a possible way of providing the lead for a small congregation to sing to.

INSTRUMENTAL MUSIC AS VOLUNTARIES

Although the organ will be the norm for most occasions, alternative forms of music can from time to time provide contrast and give variety. As with many of the matters we have discussed, this presupposes the availability of the necessary forces.

I well remember hearing a Telemann trio sonata for flute, violin and organ before the Sunday morning Eucharist at a church in Toronto. I also recall the slow movement of a Haydn string quartet played in an English church by father, mother and two daughters who, when they had finished, took their place in the choir for the service. On both occasions there was applause.

The revival of the middle voluntary is something which might be employed rather more. It was popular during the seventeenth century as a link between the psalms and the first lesson. Joseph Poole has made provision for this in some of the non-liturgical services he has devised as the basis of some of the RSCM Festival Service Books. Although the middle voluntary is seldom heard in Anglican services, the Free Churches invariably take up the collection while the congregation listen to organ music. This is a far better procedure than the Anglican custom of the collection being combined with the singing of a hymn. In many North American churches the collection is taken during the playing of organ music, or sometimes during the singing of an anthem after which, when the offertory is presented at the altar, all join in singing the doxology 'Praise God from whom all blessings flow'.

Whatever method is, or is not, adopted, there is no reason why a middle voluntary should not be played elsewhere in a service as a reflective respite from active worship. The use of these alternative forms of music in England seems to be so limited as to makes its rarity value the more memorable. This is surely a further reason for employing young people from school instrumental groups.

The practicalities of where to seat the players should generally present few problems, the chancel being the obvious place in which they can be seen, and probably heard, to advantage.

THE VOLUNTARY AS SUCH

Erik Routley has quoted Dr Nathaniel Micklem as having said that 'the introductory organ music does for Protestants what the scent of incense does for Catholics; it lifts them over the threshold of the church'.

I am not sure that this claim could be made quite so accurately today, certainly as far as the Roman Catholics are concerned, yet the value of pre-service music is significant in that it is, or should be, a mood setter. This presupposes the organist choosing with care and forethought the suitability of what will be played; this also necessitates proper rehearsal.

With the contemporary emphasis on welcoming the congregation, the family togetherness of worship and the paraphernalia of giving out the various books and leaflets which are an occupational hazard of churchgoing today, the organ voluntary can all too easily become either a cover-up for chatter or background ecclesiastical musak. This is not good enough. Given that the organist has carefully chosen and prepared the music, it is a lack of courtesy towards the player who, as I know from experience, feels discouraged by what in any other area of music making would be considered downright bad manners and, moreover, would not be tolerated by the listener.

Some of us are old fashioned enough to want to say our prayers before a service commences and to prepare ourselves quietly. Music can be an aid towards this but not when accompanied by a buzz of chatter which is invariably on matters quite unconnected with the service about to take place.

Another hazard for those of us who sit in the congregation is hearing the bells ring in one key while the organ is playing in another. This collision of sound is hardly conducive to being the mood setter referred to earlier. Surely the bell-ringers can be persuaded to stop five minutes before a service commences so that the organist can take over.

In some churches where there is a Sunday bulletin, the titles of the voluntaries are included. This helps to associate the music with the service as a whole and not as a vague extra tacked on at either end. I would plead for a more general adoption of this principle, even to the extent of the congregation being encouraged to sit and listen to the final voluntary *as part of the service* and not, as in so many instances, it being the signal for a general exodus. Having said this, it is only reasonable to suggest that the final organ music be neither too loud nor too long, as the clergy may understandably wish to speak to members of the congregation at the conclusion of a service.

I find that outside England congregations do in fact frequently stay and quietly listen to the final music and that it leads to a realization of the rightful place and function of the voluntary.

Improvising should never be entered into lightly, and certainly never as the lazy organist's excuse for not preparing a set piece. Having said this, I believe there is every justification for a measure of improvising by cathedral organists and others who are highly skilled in this respect, especially when it is a preamble to a quiet daily Evensong. As the average parish organist may not always possess the necessary skills needed to sustain the interest of the listener, a series of passing notes, modulations and suspensions within a framework of fairly predictable legato chords can all too quickly pall on the ear. When Sunday after Sunday such a sequence of events is unvarying, it fails to become that mood setter which is so essential.

THE SPOKEN PARTS OF A SERVICE

These are in many respects as relevant as the music in that all of us nowadays are involved in the total concept of worship. The age old suggestion that the task of the choir is merely to sing and, by implication, to opt out of everything else in a service is by no means entirely exploded. It is even prompted by some 'professional' choirs who view their role as being very much that of an élitist musical body for whom the business of worship, as they see it, concerns only the clergy and congregation.

The choir, together with the congregation, should provide a clear and positive lead to those parts of a service which are said. It is not, as some would have us believe, that vitality in worship will come about if everything is both loud and fast, especially in terms of the music. Neither will necessarily provide the right answer, any more than a laborious slowness in which every comma becomes a stopping place will sound any more convincing. What does matter is that clergy, choir and congregation move as one, and at a deliberate pace which takes care of phrasing and punctuation, so that everything which is said makes sense. Essential to this is the need for every word, however important or unimportant, to be clearly articulated. Similarly, ends of phrases need to be distinct and not allowed to fade away.

All of this presupposes that we are thinking about what we say. The repetitive nature of much of what we say week by week in church can so easily allow slackness and a parrot-fashion approach. How many of us can put our hand on our heart and honestly claim that every time we say the Creed and the Our Father we make it a new experience? Human nature being what it is, our minds wander and our thoughts easily become distracted by what is going on around us.

A typical example of this comes near the start of the Creed in Holy Communion Rite A where we should say 'of all that is, seen and unseen'. The comma divides this statement into two distinct parts which, if observed, summons up an entirely new and different vision from what was in the original version.

Inserted at a crucial moment in the Eucharistic Prayer we not only state that Christ has died but that he is risen (a statement fundamental to the Christian faith) and, moreover, that Christ *will* most certainly come again. These are three distinct statements in which our voices should rise in pitch, even excitement, while getting louder and more urgent. In this way our response to proclaiming the mystery of faith becomes a moment of great impact, heightened the more when the shout is

71

spontaneous, even to the extent of being untidy. This is the true meaning of 'acclamation'. There is nothing gimmicky in this, merely a particularly effective way of highlighting an essential moment in the unfolding of the drama of the Eucharist.

The reading of lessons and the leading of intercessory prayers do not strictly concern us here, except to say that any responses need to be boldly and clearly said.

How to begin corporate prayers can be inconclusive unless some policy has been agreed on. It is probably best in most circumstances for the priest to begin and for the people then to join in:

Priest: Almighty God,

People: to whom all hearts are open ...

Because it is important to get this right, it is dealt with in detail in *Music and The Alternative Service Book* (Addington Press – RSCM/Mowbray).

It is generally helpful to read from the book when saying corporate prayers. This ensures accuracy, especially in those parts where the ASB is only slightly different from what we have previously been accustomed to. However familiar prayers may be and however much we may know them from memory, it is by following the printed page that we concentrate more fully on their meaning.

In all this there is the practical consideration that choirs and, for that matter, congregations who take the trouble to articulate clearly when speaking are the more likely to do so when singing. The rhythm and vitality of vowels and consonants rub off on the singing, a matter in which singers can be notoriously lazy. The more emphasis there is on articulation the more likely will be the rhythmic vitality of the singing.

It is the clergy who regrettably are the worst offenders in speaking either too quickly or too slowly, in projecting a dull monochrome voice and in being indistinct. Would that the clergy were unfailingly taught while at theological college to project their voice, and taught to do so by a real professional. It would help a lot to take a leaf out of the book of actors, media newsreaders and airport flight announcers, all of whom have to be professional if they are to keep their jobs, even though what they have to say is never on a level with the fine prose of the Church's liturgy.

CONCLUSIONS

1. The need to emphasize that standards are important and do matter. Only the best will suffice in every aspect of music in worship. In this respect the example set by many of our English cathedrals can be used as a yardstick in terms of doing all things well.

2. It is not irrelevant to note – even though some of us may not like to admit it – the preparation and effort, and the corresponding results which often underline the music of evangelical and charismatic worship. It is by no means uncommon to experience here a vitality and polish not always automatically associated with the performance of more traditional forms of music. Maybe some of this springs from the energy and highly charged propulsion of a relatively new situation in which the person in charge of the music may not necessarily be an organist. Is there perhaps food for thought here and the need for a minister of music as opposed to the old concept of the organist as such?

In the final analysis, whatever music may be in use, the good will be as good as the bad is bad, the latter sometimes unspeakably so.

3. We have to decide what kind of music we are going to opt for in the twentieth century, a decision which will be determined by factors discussed again and again in the course of this book. We also have to bear in mind that non-traditional types of music can in performance be as dull as traditional forms presented in a dull way. It is a false premise to assume that folk, trendy or 'pop' music will automatically vitalize worship. The two poles are

indeed a long way apart in concept and therefore in performance needs. Likewise, it is necessary to emphasize that 'folk' and allied types of music imply a special idiom and that the traditionally trained church musician does not necessarily know how to cope with the unfamiliar, any more than the reverse situation will work out. The two are quite different and must be treated as such. In the same way, much of the ASB can misfire when its contents are approached and used in the same way as BCP services would be.

4. The rival claims of choir and congregation, if such they be, should not be a battle, but a carefully considered liaison.

5. I would again stress that we live in an age of challenge and opportunity within the Church, but that music must never be allowed to dominate worship in all its rich components. Music must certainly never become an embarrassment to worship, nor must it be a soft option, however much some would persuade us of this. Music, as with prayer, will demand effort and perseverance, be it the simplest hymn or the most elaborate anthem. There will inevitably be many disappointments and many frustrations; but these must not deflect us from the ultimate objective of music as an enrichment of worship.

4

THE PARSON AND THE ORGANIST – A JOINT MINISTRY?

'Lord, help us to disagree, but without being disagreeable'

(a) 'I said to my vicar, "Now let's get this straight; your job's worship and mine's the music. Let's agree to go our separate ways"'

(b) 'When I came to the parish a few months ago, I realized its worship was long overdue for a new look to give it new life. My organist seems to resist or reject out of hand, as a matter of principle, any suggestion of change. I believe he genuinely sees nothing wrong with the status quo. I certainly want to avoid a showdown, but what am I to do? He obviously feels threatened and suspects me of being "way out". I want to work with him and help him, but he is very stubborn.'

(c) 'My new vicar says he is legally in charge and, come what may, he will have what *he* wants. He never consults me over the music nor sees any viewpoint other than his own.'

(d) 'My organist plays every hymn in the same laborious and heavy way, whether it is a hymn of praise or penitence. When I ventured to comment on this, he told me he was the musical expert and more or less suggested that I mind my own business. The last straw was my suggestion that we introduce *100*

Hymns for Today. This for him was the work of the devil.'

Four extremes? Yes and no. Give or take a little, these statements ring familiar bells and are certainly no recipe for a good working relationship. They show both sides being equally difficult, and in all but one instance the problems sprang from change, either in types of worship or through the advent of a new incumbent.

AN OLD STORY
In general terms, there is little or nothing new to add to the saga of the parson/organist relationship as it specially concerns the changing situation with which this book is concerned. It is a fact that today the parson and his organist are as much as at any time in the past the two key figures around which so much revolves in public worship. The contemporary climate of events makes for greater pressures because of the fluidity of the situation. Nevertheless, both are essential to the operation and, human nature being what it is, the classic cat-and-mouse situation is just as likely to emerge today as at any time in the past.

THE RELATIONSHIP TODAY
A good working relationship is the more essential today if only because issues virtually unknown a generation ago now loom large. Changes in the shape and language of services inevitably rub off on the music and the musicians and friction can arise the more easily. Nowadays, both sides so readily feel threatened and consequently tend to react from a position of insecurity. In practice it matters not whether this threat is in fact real or imaginary.

Many clergy genuinely wish, and with good cause, to rethink or 'renew' worship. This can range from a mild reordering of certain aspects to something approaching a radical reassessment. Any use of the word renewal is almost certain to lead to suspicion in some quarters; it can all too readily be a 'dirty word' and loaded with foreboding of what might result. The incidence of soured parson/organist relationships so often results from the introduction of new services, which in themselves ought to be the occasion and the opportunity for presenting new life and new thought into a parish.

Organists sometimes see change triggered off by the introduction of the ASB as something which by its very nature will of necessity minimize and even ultimately erode the musical content of the services. They therefore fight to safeguard the music, and for this they must be applauded. There have been more than a few fleeting instances where the new services have been made the excuse for deliberately forcing out the music, and not always because the organist and choir have been reluctant to accept change.

The extent of the togetherness which characterizes much of the present day worship scene must be worked out, and by all concerned, so that by mutual agreement and trust an agreed dosage can be arrived at. This is seldom likely to be the same in any two parishes, for the traditions, needs and, not least, the available musical resources will be fundamental contributory factors. *What works, and is needed, in one situation may be entirely unsuitable in another*. Even so, arriving at fair shares for all takes tact and diplomacy, in which parson and organist play a prominent role.

When *both* parties respect and trust each other, are willing to see the other point of view and, if necessary, to compromise, the chances are that decisions will be arrived at which are likely to be in the best interests of all. It is when relationships are soured and both parties are bent on scoring off each other that the wrong answers are likely to emerge and, from these, the Church will suffer.

Not least in all this is the power of prayer, for, as

Tennyson so aptly reminds us, 'More things are wrought by prayer than this world dreams of'.

A JOINT MINISTRY?

This it *must* be. Neither parson nor organist can properly, or ideally, function without the other. It is as simple as that. When this joint ministry is made to work, the one aids and complements the ministry of the other – and it is a two-way traffic. Between them they will to a considerable extent not only determine what happens Sunday by Sunday, but also between them jointly enrich the entire concept and completeness of worship to a degree impossible when one or other acts singly or, worse still, in opposition.

The real problem is that while there are some very difficult, truculent and 'dog in the manger' organists around, there are also some autocratic clergy in circulation, some of whom have confused their authority with autocracy. Further tensions can arise when an organist is either an unbeliever or lukewarm in Christian commitment, while the parson, for his part, may not be interested in music and will let this be known.

An additional problem can arise from the fact that each works separately for six days of the week, and they probably only meet each Sunday for the purpose of working together. The preparatory work of each is done in private and often in isolation, yet it sees its fulfilment in public worship where no holds are barred. How important it is to have a weekly staff meeting for all who are in any way concerned with the preparation and presentation of Sunday worship.

The fact that in many instances this particular relationship does work is not only borne out by the results but is testimony to the mutual trust the one has for the other. In other words it can, and does, work.

I would go so far as to say that where the ordering of public worship is concerned, clergy/organist relationships are prob-

ably more crucial than any other single factor.

As I move around, not only in Britain but throughout much of the English speaking world, I gain experience of both sides of this particular coin. If, as a result, I adopted the media policy of highlighting only bad news as being of interest, I would soon arrive at distorted conclusions. The fact is that one hears more of situations which are unstable or explosive than of those churches where all is well. I feel that some consideration of the viewpoints, together with the pros and cons governing opposing attitudes, is called for and from which solutions may be forthcoming in a constructive way.

AS IT AFFECTS THE CLERGY

1. The need to acknowledge the place and role of music as an integral part of worship. Music has always had a prominence in Christian worship and most would agree that the Church would be greatly impoverished should the day ever dawn when music ceased to fulfil that role. I find it hard to understand clergy who view music, and especially the choir, as a threat. A threat to what? Is it that music can sometimes show up the inadequacy of the clergy? Music can surely only become a threat if it is allowed to get out of control, to assume too great a prominence or do a take-over bid.

A choir should surely be used both in its own right, in what it can contribute to worship, and also to lead the worship through music. Conversely, it should not be underemployed. Arriving at the right answer for each and every situation will involve consultation, not only between the clergy and the musicians but also with the congregation, those long suffering people on the receiving end whose point of view should always be taken into account.

Given that the right answers have been arrived at – and these may not necessarily emerge overnight – music can add so much to the totality of the ministry of the clergy.

2. Inbred fear of establishment worship can so easily lead to the taking of wrong turnings which in their turn result in excesses in one form or another. 'Our new vicar wants to change everything', is so often heard said as to be of more than casual significance. To build on what one inherits, and maybe to make certain changes in the process is one thing, but to attempt radically to alter virtually everything within weeks of arriving in a parish, can signal immediate and very real problems. In such circumstances the vicar becomes a marked man and a collision course inevitable. While there may be need for change, support for it is more likely to be forthcoming if moves are made gradually and with consultation at all stages, linked with a full understanding by all concerned as to what is envisaged.

While a new incumbent may feel it his mission to make musical changes, this should always be approached tactfully, bearing in mind that the organist has probably been in office for some years and understandably resents bulldozing tactics by a newcomer. One of the biggest crosses any organist has to bear is the parson who *thinks* he knows all about music and is opinionated on the subject. It is surely not asking too much to suggest that a balance be aimed at.

I put these points in the hope that they may help in avoiding a situation too frequently encountered nowadays where the arrival of a new incumbent too often heralds the demise of the choir and the resultant decline of the music, the ultimate being either the resignation or dismissal of the organist. The advent of a new incumbent should surely give new life and vision to the musicians, and will do so if approached in the right way.

3. *The choosing of hymns*. Nothing is more frustrating for a conscientious organist than to be given the hymns for next Sunday at the last possible moment, sometimes even too late for them to be rehearsed by the choir.

In a similar way, some clergy have the infuriating habit

of deciding to change the final hymn during the course of the service. Both are examples of bad administration and show a lack of businesslike efficiency. How much better when hymns are chosen jointly by parson and organist with each adding his expertise to that of the other. In this way the chances are that a better choice will emerge with, as part of the process, parson and organist perhaps learning a little more of what makes the other tick.

4. The co-opting of the organist on to the PCC can be a valuable move. It is encouraging to hear of more and more instances where this is now the norm. Through this the organist can contribute a full, and official, part to the overall life of his church and parish.

5. Some clergy claim that folk music and 'pop' are the art of the people and that traditional church music is a very small part of the overall picture. Fair enough, but there is also the question of suitability, and that previously mentioned point of small being sometimes beautiful. It could of course be that clergy conditioned to a weekly diet of turgid and lifeless hymn playing are driven, if only through sheer desperation, to seek new avenues. Whether or not they find the right answer is another matter.

6. What of the parson who cannot comprehend what music can add to the completeness of worship? Could it be that he has never fully experienced this? Suffice it to say that a lack of appreciation by clergy and congregations for the efforts of their musicians can all too easily make an organist tempt fate and go one step too far, if only through sheer frustration.

7. Also, what of the church where infinite pains are taken to see that the neatness and cleanliness of the building, its flowers, its vestments and other adornments are of the highest possible standard, yet which at the same time can subscribe to the belief that the more spontaneous, off-the-cuff, unrehearsed and informal the music is, so much the better? The reasoning which dictates that the music, no matter how badly prepared and performed, will be *per*

81

se acceptable to the Almighty, seems an illogical reasoning. Surely every aspect of worship, be it visual or aural, demands effort and, in the event, is experienced to the fullest as a result of that effort.

AS IT AFFECTS THE MUSICIANS

1. The organist has a responsibility for the conduct of services equal to that of the clergy. This applies not only to the music but also to the said parts, while the overall pace of a service concerns the organist and choir as much as the clergy. Once again it is surely a matter of doing *all* things well.

2. The organist should always have in mind that music is the handmaid of religion. To this end he should never subscribe towards encouraging or allowing anything savouring of a liturgical concert.

3. Leading on from this, I believe that every organist and choir director should have a basic knowledge of liturgy, what exactly it is and how and why we have arrived at the point at which we find ourselves today, not only in the Anglican church but throughout the whole of Christendom. Some knowledge of theology, however elementary, can be of equal value in helping a musician to understand better the nature and purpose of worship. An awareness of the historical growth of hymnody, not least the words, will make a church musician the better informed in a major aspect of his work.

Sometimes an organist who is musically qualified up to the hilt cannot relate to the clergy because he is deficient in these other respects. A knowledge of liturgy, theology and hymnody therefore helps him to be more able to talk on equal terms with the clergy.

4. It follows that to be a complete church musician one must be a practising Christian. This would perhaps seem to be stating the obvious, but the evidence does not always support this. Merely glance back at the quotes which opened this chapter as proof of this.

Where the organist is a convinced and practising Christian this will be reflected in that extra something which, although difficult to define, marks out the organ playing and the work of a choir in a special and distinctive way.

5. The choir and organist can through their support and friendship be of immense help and encouragement to the clergy, who in their turn are the more likely to reciprocate. Once again it's a two way traffic – and – we are all in it together.

THE JOINT TASK – INCLUDING A RECAPITULATION OF THINGS SAID EARLIER

1. If both parties try to understand each other's point of view they are the more likely to arrive at a happy working relationship.

2. Linked with this is the need for constant consultation, with joint meetings on matters of interest and mutual concern. Lack of this will only lead to suspicion as to the motives of the other. A feeling of security and mutual trust is therefore needed *on both sides*.

3. Each must recognize that there are diversities of gifts and that allowance must be made for this. In itself, such diversity can be a broadening and enriching experience.

4. It is as unrealistic to suggest that contemporary worship should deny any reference to the past as it is to look on all things pre-1950 as sacrosanct. There are things old and new in our treasure store, which parson and organist must recognize as having an individual validity to each and every situation.

5. The ill effects of jealousy, and all that emanates from this pernicious attribute, are no less rife in church circles than in any other walk of life.

6. Try to avoid being unpredictable which, after all, is only a pose.

7. While some clergy experience a genuine frustration from an 'establishment' situation and therefore tend to

react against establishment musicians, some organists are rigidly and immovably persuaded that they have much to stand up for in retarding on principle any genuine moves forward.

8. Work out how best to make the pre-service voluntary a genuine mood setter. It should act as a preparation and never be merely ecclesiastical musak. Similarly, at the end of a service, a buzz of conversation immediately the concluding organ music begins is distracting, even insulting, to the player.

9. In the same way that clergy attend retreats and conferences from which they return to their parish with new incentives and probably with a shot-in-the-arm, so should the organist and choir director be encouraged from time to time to attend courses which will similarly recharge him. Is it too much to ask that the church pay for, or contribute towards, the cost of such a course? As organists are seldom paid a realistic remuneration this could be a way of saying thank you.

10. The devil you know, warts and all, is preferable to the alternative of being without an organist and with little reasonable hope of finding a suitable replacement. The demand today far exceeds the supply. Many who might in the past have taken a regular church appointment do not do so nowadays, either because they, or their family, want weekend mobility and freedom, or because they are soured through having experienced bad working relationships with the clergy. Too many organists become dispirited and disillusioned, and not infrequently opt in the last resort to resigning. This usually means that they and their talents are lost to the Church for ever. Relatively few of those who leave under strained circumstances ever take on another post.

Although an incumbent may at present be within his legal rights to dismiss his organist, how much better if he looks on his organist as his friend, and not as his enemy. Such a policy can pay handsome dividends on both sides, not least in helping to soften the heart of the toughest musician.

Not unconnected with this is the case of the parson who finds it difficult to relate to his organist and work with him, sometimes to such an extent that no one stays for any length of time in his employ. In such circumstances the word soon gets around and he ultimately finds it hard, if not impossible, to entice anyone to take on the post.

11. *An irreparable breakdown in relationships does no one any good and certainly gets neither party anywhere.*

12. There is a joint responsibility for ensuring vitality in worship. Sometimes our ecclesiastical restraint disallows this – or else we go overboard and chase false hares which have no lasting value or permanency.

SOME SUGGESTED REMEDIES

1. Music and musicians are an inescapable part of the responsibility of the clergy. While a parson need not necessarily be musical as such, he cannot, unless he has no conscience in the matter, opt out of his duty to view music as part of his overall parochial ministry. Furthermore, although he may not perhaps like music, he must not make that the excuse for denying it to others, any more than the fact that he may not happen to like a certain hymn is a reason for prohibiting its use. The same applies to organists who adopt a similar attitude.

2. When parson and organist fall out with each other, as in any breakdown in relationships, there will probably be faults on both sides. What should never happen is for either side to allow a situation to deteriorate into permanent deadlock from which there is no point of return. The problem is that when it comes to the crunch, the organist has far less bargaining power than the parson – and the wily parson knows this.

3. I would suggest that 'director of music' or better still 'minister of music', is sometimes a more accurate job

description than 'organist'. It is certainly more embracing and could help promote a wider view.

To end on a positive note, where common sense prevails, as it does in many instances, and where mutual trust and respect operate, it is abundantly possible to make the parson/organist situation a viable proposition. This, moreover, can be achieved through the will to ensure that the partnership is an effective one even if in the process some compromise is necessary, probably even desirable. Compromise is, after all, no bad thing in itself, especially when it leads to a better end product without either party having to abrogate principles or credibility.

I would reiterate that this relationship can all too easily become a sensitive issue, with both sides having much to answer for. It is for this reason that I have discussed its ramifications at some length.

A final thought. Fear is the evil one's long range weapon, because beyond almost all anger lies fear.

POSTSCRIPT
Because I am a musician it could be thought that I view music in worship solely from the musicians' side of the fence. I hope that my track record over the years shows this not to be. The fact that for the past ten years I have not been an organist and therefore go to church each Sunday as a member of the congregation, gives me a reasonably clear picture of the other side. Having said this, I am forced to admit (even at the risk of being branded a clergy baiter – which I am not) that there are far too many instances of clergy giving music short value and the musicians less than fair treatment, sometimes to the extent of organists being dismissed in a cavalier, insensitive and even sub-Christian way – and without the normally accepted processes of consultation and discussion. This is something which would never be tolerated in other walks of life. Such situations not only produce

media publicity, but can all too easily result in a situation in which young and old alike become thoroughly disillusioned and sometimes even lost to the Church. Worship then becomes divisive rather than the unifying force it should be.

5

SOME IMPORTANT INCIDENTALS

CHURCHES WITHOUT CHOIRS

This is a relatively new phenomenon and one of the many results of the changing situation affecting the Church.

A church without a choir does not of necessity mean a church without music. Far from it. In the past we have invariably assumed this, usually because in the Anglican Church we have taken choirs for granted. There are now many instances where, for one reason or another, it is neither possible nor practicable to have a choir, certainly an SATB one. We must therefore cut our cloth accordingly; but – this does not imply that what we end up with is of necessity second best.

Such is the extent of the situation that the RSCM is actively considering a new category of membership specifically aimed at helping those churches without a choir. It has often been claimed that because a church has no choir there is little point in being affiliated to the RSCM. This points to something being radically wrong if membership hinges solely on the existence of a choir.

In general, there would seem to be three categories which should claim our attention:

1. The church where there is no choir because the resources are simply not available, even though they may have been in the past. Alternatives have therefore to be sought. In such circumstances we need to consider how to adapt existing music for choirless churches, how to use the congregation to the fullest possible advantage, how to

help clergy and organists to prepare services in such a situation, and how to explore the possible use of musical leaders from within the congregation to act as cantors. Not least, there needs to be discussion on what possibilities might perhaps exist for the formation of a group of singers, however small or basic, who could act as a choir.

2. The situation where the role of the choir is deliberately played down or minimized because the ASB is in use. In such cases there is sometimes something of a conspiracy highlighting the congregational aspect of worship, while off-loading and unfairly relegating the choir to a position little more than that of being there under sufferance.

3. Those churches where a choir is not considered necessary or even desirable. While this can come about because the track record of a choir was such as to make it become a liability to worship, sometimes it happens that, when a parish experiences 'renewal', it is taken for granted that the church will have automatically moved away from a traditional choir situation. This is an arrogant assumption with little or nothing to substantiate or warrant it. How much better if a church, so renewed in its worship, takes along with it the best of the old rather than automatically discarding it.

This type of situation is the most difficult of the three and the one most calculated to bring problems. In such circumstances, do-it-yourself types of chorus may at first seem to be the answer, but the novelty value can very quickly wear thin, as can the mundane repetitiveness of the words and music of many choruses.

The snag in many such situations is that permanency is sometimes considered to be one of the ugly words of today; but this is surely only valid if it leads to stagnation.

Choir or no choir, we should have no illusions, nor should we be unduly influenced by the thinking which dictates that if a choir is present the congregation will not sing. The fact is that even when there is no choir there is no automatic guarantee that the congregation will sing, this because Anglican parish worship is conditioned to the presence of a choir. This has proved to be a very good and useful inbuilt feature in the growth and development of Anglican worship, especially during the past century.

The belief, however fashionable in some quarters, that if you dispense with the choir the congregation will take on a more active musical role is not borne out by the results. The pews are still half empty.

If there is no choir, the logical deduction is that there will be no leadership in the singing. Therefore, when we are faced with such a situation, we should cultivate an element of congregational singing in its own right. In this context we might well consider the Free Churches who place comparatively little reliance on the choir, where there are few anthems or additional choir material, and where the resulting musical diet is a simple one resting mainly on the use of hymnody.

One of the special features of RSCM help for churches without choirs is that of training organists to lead the singing in the special way needed, which is a very different proposition from when a choir is present.

We acknowledge that it is much harder to help in the choirless situation. Perhaps here we should, as in other situations, ponder the relevance of the prayer which suggests that we have the courage to change the things we can change, the serenity to accept those we cannot change 'and the wisdom to know the difference'.

THE CHOIR – ROBED OR NOT?

As with so many things, this is a feature of Anglicanism which, although highly valued in many instances, is liable nowadays to come under scrutiny and certainly to be questioned.

The main argument used against having a robed choir is that it can be divisive and serve merely to heighten any physical or geographical separation which already exists between choir and congregation. The physical separation of choir and congregation was commented on in Chapter 2 and the problem it can raise when Rite A Holy Communion is in use, though this applies whether a choir is robed or not.

A further argument concerning the robed choir is that it increases the possibility of the élitism which is such a fearful bogey for some.

The case for having a robed choir can be justified on a number of counts, the main one being that it is a known fact that a uniformly dressed choir generally tends to sing with a greater feeling of being a unit or a team. The concept of the team is a particularly valid one for young people. In a similar way a football team wears a distinctive uniform by which it is identified in much the same way as the clerical collar singles out the parson. The catalogue of uniforms is endless and extends even to the gear of skinheads and punks. At some time or another we all revel in dressing up for a special occasion. What better than for churchgoing?

What a robed choir actually wears is another matter. Cassock and surplice, which is essentially a male outfit, can be a cumbersome partnership unless tailormade for the individual. With the addition of the ruff for children there is a sizable and time-consuming laundering exercise for someone. As an alternative, there is much to be said for a unisex garment, the most popular being of bleached linen with a corded girdle. Most suppliers will be able to suggest suitable designs. The net result is probably far more practicable, and certainly more edifying, than surplices and ruffs which after two or three wearings can look tired and untidy.

You have only to look on a sea of choirs, as I so often do when conducting a choral festival, to marvel at the strange diversity of garb some choirs come up with, not least the headgear of the ladies.

Some type of robe also covers a multitude of sins in that it hides tee shirts and, if long enough, the inevitable jeans. Footwear is another matter and, unless suitable, can look strangely out of keeping, especially when trainers protrude under a cassock.

There may be very good reasons why a choir is not robed, not least being the expense factor. There is no reason why an unrobed choir cannot look tidy especially when, as in most instances, they dress identically in much the same way as would a choral society. Those dolled up to the nines sometimes tend to look down on their unrobed friends as inferior beings. Being unrobed is certainly not a second class situation.

In the often casually dressed world in which we live, not all would agree with these comments; nevertheless, there is the visual aspect from the congregation's point of view which should be taken into account. A tidily turned out choir can be an aid to worship in the same way that an ill assorted assembly can be distinctly off-putting.

All in all, the matter of robing is a questionable one. If it helps to be robed and if it looks seemly, all well and good. If it does not help then an alternative must be found. The main consideration is to leave well alone. If it is the custom and tradition to robe, why run the risk of alienating people by altering it?

MUSIC IN FAMILY SERVICES

The basic problem here is how to cater for all needs. Perhaps it is an over-simplification to suggest that if you have music suitable for the children, then the adults will be unfulfilled, and certainly vice versa.

It has been suggested by the Revd Michael Perham, Secretary of the Church of England Doctrine Commission, that family services can be a useful introduction to liturgical worship, provided they are used as a bridge. He goes on to say that there is therefore good reason for using certain excerpts, such as Gloria and Sanctus, by way of an introduction to the Eucharist.

Shape and development are important factors here. As with all free structured services, it is so easy literally to go as the spirit moves one. Few can steer this approach successfully without some guidelines. All too often such services can become nebulous and lack the focal points which occur in the unfolding of the drama of the Eucharist as compared with Morning and Evening Prayer which by their very nature are much more static.

A further point in working out the content of family services is the matter of participation. Here, as in ASB services, this has to be carefully worked out so that not everyone is involved in doing everything all the time. Otherwise the pursuit of prayer becomes restless and unabating.

PAY AND WORKING CONDITIONS – ORGANISTS

The Incorporated Society of Musicians issues a comprehensive guide on the subject. It costs 65p and is obtainable either from them at 10 Stratford Place, London W1N 9AE, or from the RSCM. It contains detailed information ranging from village church organists to the cathedrals and covers every aspect of the subject. The RSCM amplifies the parish part of this through a leaflet giving guidelines on suggested minimum rates of remuneration for organists in the three main categories:

1. the small village or suburban church with simple services and probably no choir;
2. larger village or suburban churches having a choir and one rehearsal per week;
3. town churches having two rehearsals per week.

Whatever category applies, it must be recognized that we live in an inflationary age and that any remuneration should be reviewed annually. Whatever figure may be arrived at, few, if any of us, who work for the Church expect to be in the top income bracket. Even so, the labourer is worthy of his or her hire and should not necessarily be expected to be out of pocket. In the final reckoning, much of what is paid will anyhow go towards car and telephone expenses and the like.

As individual financial circumstances vary greatly, each case will obviously need to be worked out on its own merits by employer and employee and with these matters in mind.

SECURITY OF TENURE

An RSCM working party is currently engaged at looking into this often troubled area which is being increasingly highlighted through the all too frequent summary dismissal of the organist by the incumbent. The working party has stressed how essential it is for the appointment of an organist to be subject to an agreement in writing, which must reflect the present law in regard to appointment and dismissal. When difficulties arise, both sides frequently take up entrenched positions.

While an incumbent has the undisputed right and duty to guide worship in ways that will best help the parishioners – though this does not imply it being at the expense of the music – there is nowadays, as we have noted earlier, a far greater emphasis on congregational participation. As a result, such matters as informal music as opposed to more traditional types can become focal points of dispute. What does seem unjust is that when an incumbent wishes to make changes he can, if he feels his organist is an obstacle to this, summarily dismiss him, and with no right of appeal. Not surprisingly, clergy are, as a whole, sensitive on this issue while organists for their part are incensed. It is hoped that a *modus vivendi* can, and will, be arrived at. This is surely not impossible provided there is a measure of give and take on both sides.

THE PAYMENT OF CHOIRS

While in most parishes amateur adult singers are seldom paid, children come into a somewhat different category. This cannot be easily worked out in terms which will suffice for all cases, for a number of points need to be taken into account.

Payment should never be regarded as a rightful entitlement. The work of a chorister is best approached by each individual as his or her offering of time and talent towards the enrichment of the worship of the church. Where some form of payment is in operation, it is surely more appropriate that this be looked on as pocket money rather than pay given by the church as a reward for services rendered.

There are some instances of a reverse procedure, with choristers voluntarily giving a percentage of what they receive to a special fund set up for the benefit of the choir as a whole, such as towards choir outings, fees for courses, even sometimes towards the cost of music and robes. If rightly approached and explained to a choir, this can make the members appreciate the more their membership and commitment.

Any payment is usually made at quarterly or half yearly intervals. How this is arrived at in specific sums of money will obviously be determined by available funds, length of service and seniority, with the latter being earned and not arrived at automatically. Whatever the answer, it is unlikely to compare favourably with what can be earned for such part-time employment as delivering newspapers or some similar task, though it is to be hoped that the job satisfaction of singing in a church choir will far outweigh monetary considerations.

For boy choristers an alternative can be for one half of what has been earned to be credited to a savings account, the sum total with interest being handed over at the end of his time as a treble. For those who may have some reservations about the giving of money, a book prize or book token could be given as an annual gift from the church with its presentation made publicly at a service.

Payment for weddings and other special services comes into a different category and cannot be reasonably criticized.

While adults usually understand more readily the concept of service, children cannot necessarily be expected to see it in quite the same way.

Perhaps more important than payment is the mere fact of being in a good choir and the training this brings. At its best there is the experience of doing this particular kind of work during young and impressionable years, and the discipline (however dirty a word that may be today) being as much a contributory factor and as much a reality now as at any time in the past. Being treated in similar terms as the adult members of a choir in that much is expected of each and every member, and the fact that each week the choir 'performs' in public, are additional bonuses. It is interesting to find the percentage of clergy who were boy choristers and are grateful for the training and experience it brought.

Whether it be boys or girls, it must be stressed that the question of payment should not be viewed as being something of right even though the adult world at large views this rather differently. A wise choir director will see that this matter is kept within its correct proportions.

As a help, the RSCM issue a leaflet entitled 'Monetary Rewards for Junior Choristers'.

ON ORGANS

Every so often comes the time when work other than general maintenance needs to be carried out. As the organ is probably the largest and most expensive single piece of furniture in a church, great care needs to be exercised in doing the right thing, not only for the present but for the benefit of the future. The incumbent and the PCC as custodians of the church are therefore responsible for the organ.

Firstly, do take advice, and reliable expert advice. This is relatively easy to come by, the three main sources being your Diocesan Organ Adviser, the Organs Advisory Committee (which is one of the official committees set up by the Church of England as part of the Council for the Care of Churches), and the RSCM. As with the BBC's Antique Road Show, there are plenty of authorities willing and able to assess a situation and to give advice on how best to proceed.

Do you rebuild or, in a world so governed by electronics, automatically look for an electronic substitute? In many instances a case can be made for or against either course of action; not all pipe organs are good nor are all electronics bad. Expediency is of the essence and no binding decision should be taken lightly, nor on the advice of a member of the PCC who may be something of an electronics expert and as a consequence very persuasive in that direction.

While there have been immense advances in electronic organs they still remain substitutes for the real thing. That means balancing authentic sound against something produced by other, and sometimes less satisfactory, means which, as experience has shown, can pall on the ear after a while.

Never be persuaded that an electronic instrument will automatically be cheaper, with no maintenance or other problems once it is installed. The public house or drawing room model may be relatively inexpensive and, while suitable for what it is intended for, is not the answer for a comparatively large church and the function it will be expected to fulfil.

We need not enter here into detailed pros and cons. It has all been said before and so often; yet both sides continue to take up entrenched positions as advocates. The only really satisfactory answer is to seek impartial advice from expert sources; but, when coming to a decision, remember that you will only get what you are prepared to pay for. If one estimate is considerably lower than another, and both specify the same work, you can be sure someone is undercutting and that the finished product will reflect this. In these days of economic stringency no one organ builder can be all that much cheaper than another unless he is offering less value for money. Sharp practices in organ building are no less prevalent than in other areas.

The Organs Advisory Committee (Council for the Care of Churches, 83 London Wall, London EC2M 5NA) have produced two useful pamphlets, one on *Electronic Organs* and the other a general policy statement.

Whether or not restoration work needs to be immediately undertaken, every church ought as part of its good housekeeping to initiate a sinking fund for the organ. Sooner or later the time will come when a considerable amount of money will need to be spent on an organ; this will be a highly specialist and time consuming task undertaken by a relatively small group of craftsmen working in a very expensive field to produce a custom made commodity.

Confronted with a probable estimate for some thousands of pounds, it is little wonder that a PCC takes fright. To this may be added the question whether such a sum of money is justified when the third world needs so much – though it is doubtful whether such a sum would be specially raised by a parish for this purpose in default of the organ.

A further consideration could be that many organs are too large both in size and volume. Even so, when a rebuild is envisaged it frequently follows that the organist wants the instrument to be enlarged. Seldom, if ever, is this justified. A reduction in size which takes modern voicing methods into account can usually produce a more effective result, and at less cost.

In the final analysis, much of what is decided on should fundamentally take into account the need to be good stewards and custodians of what we elect to hand on, or fail to hand on, to future generations. As the finished article is likely to be in use and therefore influence worship for a long time, it is the more necessary to seek proper advice and to heed it.

In any event, always ensure that the organ is regularly tuned and maintained in the same way that a wise motorist ensures that his car is regularly serviced.

ON CATHEDRALS

Cathedrals are, for a number of reasons, relevant to the subject matter of this book. Not the least reason is that cathedrals are able to experiment in a way not possible in most parish churches. They can try out new types of service and can do so without the constraint of a PCC. Some of this concept of being an experimental arena can be of value to the parishes whose clergy and laity can take note of and experience, if not directly emulate, such experiments.

Many of the cathedrals have broadened their ideas and witness to a remarkable degree during the past thirty years and, in the process, have become far more flexible and accessible. While a few still choose to project a Barchester-like image, either by accident or deliberately, most now have an entirely new ethos and image. In this, the older and major cathedrals have a special role which is distinctive in many ways from their newer parish church counterparts.

Our cathedrals project one of the many faces of the Church of England, in this instance the centrality of the Sunday Eucharist. For this, as for the weekday choral services, they have all the necessary resources readily laid on in a way denied to many parish churches. The musical possibilities, which ought anyhow to be on a different plane from those in the parishes, the space to emphasize the visual aspect of worship, the incomparable architecture and the aura of centuries of the daily round of Christian worship and offering, all combine to produce something unique which is totally valid as part of the overall picture.

Although cathedrals may draw relatively limited numbers as compared with a parish church (there are after all only forty-three cathedrals in England) and although the congregational involvement will be more limited than in a parish, this is by design and is balanced by other factors not applicable to the parish church. Those who opt to worship in a cathedral do so precisely because this is the type of worship they want. The fact that the regular Sunday congregations in our cathedrals, as distinct from those who attend as casual visitors, are on the increase bears this out and shows, moreover, that cathedrals today are fulfilling a need which was not generally there in the past. Even if this is not the type of worship some of us want, we must respect the fact that for others it is exactly what they need and that here they find a spirituality in which music plays a prominent part.

Nor is this confined solely to Sundays. It is also experienced in diocesan and other big services on occasions such as the Synod and ordinations, when parishioners come in from the diocese to their mother church for a great and special event full of splendour. And why not? They hear fine music sung by *their* cathedral choir, not the Merbecke or other setting they will hear week by week in their own parish. Many will subscribe once in a while to being relatively silent participants for much of the service; through this they may experience something of the transcendent and the numinous, which is no bad thing. Perhaps, as a result, they may go back and not say 'Thank God that's over' but take home one or two new ideas which could conceivably be relevant to their parish situation. They may also have been uplifted, enriched and fulfilled in the process.

Cathedrals can therefore provide for the parishes a significant yardstick in many respects, with links being forged and in many instances growing in a most rewarding and often exciting way. The resultant feedback can be a bonus to all concerned, not least in the constantly growing traffic of parish church choirs who come to their cathedral to sing choral Evensong and, in doing so, are able to spread their musical wings and so gain in experience, incentive and inspiration.

A further way in which our cathedrals are being more and more used is for concerts. There is nothing new in this as they have for centuries been used in this special way, from medieval miracle plays to their modern counterparts such as the church operas and parables of Benjamin Britten, which were conceived with the ready-made back-cloth of architectural splendour acting as a visual counterpart to the music and action.

How much better this is than the clinical concert hall. Even if the seats are harder it is a small price to pay for such a setting, for music heard in the visual and acoustic atmosphere of our cathedrals can take on an entirely new dimension. Sir John Barbirolli once said to me after conducting Vaughan Williams' *Fantasia on a theme of Thomas Tallis* in Exeter Cathedral that music such as this 'grows out of the stones of a great medieval cathedral, and when it's finished it goes back into the stones again'.

This ancillary use of churches is not confined merely to the cathedrals. It is something which in recent years has in the parish scene grown in a remarkable way, with a wide and often visionary programme content ranging from small scale local efforts to the appearance of top ranking international performers, the latter sometimes sponsored by big business.

MAKING USE OF THE RSCM

This book is in many respects a resource document in which I have not only pointed out certain matters but, more importantly, I have tried to indicate how to set about getting help and advice.

On an overall and general front, the RSCM is a worldwide resource centre, its basic task being to help and encourage all who are in any way concerned with church music. This is as true today, if not more so, than at any other time in more than fifty years of existence. During that time the RSCM has accumulated a great deal of experience not least as a result of the shifting quicksands of recent years.

Firstly, the RSCM is not what many believe, namely that we are an exclusively Church of England organization. We are fully ecumenical and have been for almost twenty years. Nor are we only concerned, as some would have it, with boy choristers and robed SATB choirs singing cathedral-type Evensong. Although these are all part of our brief, this is only in relation to what is a far wider and, by intention, all embracing outlook.

We live with this misconception, and how hard it is to dispel it. Similarly, although this particular book is by intention concerned basically with the ASB aspect and all that stems from this, the RSCM is equally ready to help those churches using the BCP – and does.

RSCM help is forthcoming in a number of ways, all of which are unique to the organization. Membership at national level, whether it be the affiliation of a church or personally as a Friend of the RSCM, keeps members in touch, not least through *Church Music Quarterly* which contains a wide spectrum of information and is sent to members four times a year. There is also a mail order service for publications with over 300 items of music, books and other instructional aids in the catalogue. Much of this comes to members with a discount of fifty per cent.

At local level, teaching events are arranged for organists, choir directors, choirs, clergy and congregations. Choral festivals are a regular means of helping choirs *en masse* and of broadening sights, with the sense of occasion foremost as the basis. On the broadly social side, events such as 'Meet, Eat and Sing' which combine a buffet meal with an opportunity informally to sing through and get to know new RSCM publications, are a popular feature not only in Britain but in many parts of the world.

At the RSCM headquarters at Addington Palace near Croydon, more than sixty courses take place each year covering every conceivable aspect of the church music scene from the traditional to the not so traditional. These range from one day events to six weeks each summer, when forty-two students from different parts of the world come for a demanding and practical insight into what church music today is all about.

In addition to all this, fourteen residential courses for boys, girls and adults are held annually at schools and colleges throughout the country and cater for the needs of over 1500 young people.

One of the most popular courses, and one for which there is never a shortage of takers, is for 'The Reluctant Organist' – the pianist recruited to play on Sundays because there is no one else available. In short courses we train pianists to come to terms with the organ, which probably means doing so without using your feet. The fact that, however many of these courses we promote, they are invariably over-subscribed, would seem to indicate the need for this particular type of help in a situation which was non-existent a few years ago when there were far more organists available and in circulation than today.

In all we do, we aim to provide help for some of the pressing needs of today which, we venture to suggest, would without our help leave many people even more confused, ill-informed and looking for help, advice and encouragement than they are.

Every member of the RSCM has the right to expect

something in return for membership. Whether this is taken up or not is another matter. Some are reluctant to come forward, either because they do not wish to show up their shortcomings, or – and these are the most difficult to help – because they think they know all the answers. Experience shows that these are the people who probably need the help, the new look, and the shot-in-the-arm, more than anyone else.

For the many who genuinely want help but are reticent in coming forward, all one can say is how good it is when such persons take the plunge and find it far less traumatic than was anticipated; and this frequently happens because they find encouragement in the fact that many on the course are far less skilled than they are.

In the end, ideal membership is not mere spectatorship. It gives a sense of belonging, and in company with others. From it you get as much or as little as you wish.

6

THE WAY AHEAD?

THOUGHTS – AND SUGGESTIONS

1. First, and perhaps foremost, is *the need for vitality in worship*. How are we to achieve this? Whether it be in the said parts where clergy, choir and congregation can all be equally guilty of an unreal and monotonous parsonic drawl, or in the sung parts where organists and choirs can be, and frequently are, responsible for no less lack of overall vitality, we so often escape the joy which, as Donald Swann once remarked, ought to be at the root of all our worship. Jeremy Taylor, the seventeenth century divine, neatly summed it up when he suggested that 'joy is the perfectest convoy for religion'.

There is much dullness in public worship and not least in the music, to which many of us at some time or another contribute. It is ironic to reflect that, for this very reason if for no other, an otherwise rationally minded parson can so easily go overboard or berserk.

2. *The attitude of 'the Church'*. Here we too often face a confused situation with thinking and principles, however well intentioned, placing the traditionalists against the radicals. Whichever way we view it, there is always the very real danger of trying to please everyone and probably ending up satisfying nobody. This is a particularly dangerous preoccupation when it comes to the music, especially when an insistence on the hogging of the lowest common denominator, which seems to be as much a feature of life within the Church as elsewhere, results in the cheap and tawdry. Worship as such, as was emphasized earlier, demands effort no less than the

music, and this goes hand in hand with the need for agreed standards of validity and integrity.

I would reiterate that I believe many of the clergy are confused over the precise role of music in worship and that, because of this, many are all to readily dedicated to being 'with it'. This, alas, is not necessarily the panacea for all ills.

3. Arising from this is the need to relieve *the tensions which can all too easily spring from the new thinking*. We sometimes fail to see the proverbial wood for the trees. It could be argued, and with some force, that there is far too much obsession with implied threat; a resulting reaction is to cling to the status quo as a means of grasping the security of the known while fearing what the unknown may hold in store.

While this is one aspect, it is not the only one. What we ideally need is a rational and considered approach which will help deter us from pursuing what might otherwise be blind alleys.

4. *The ecumenical approach*. Music speaks a common language which ideally knows few of the barriers created by differences in theology and doctrine. I believe we have as yet only begun to scratch the surface of this, and that music is a far greater pointer than we have so far realized in our quest for unity, which, incidentally, is not the same as uniformity.

5. We also need to take into account more fully *the concept of worship as being fair shares for all*. I have experienced this in widely varying circumstances. St James' Cathedral, Toronto, All Souls, Langham Place, London and the Church of St Thomas of Canterbury in Salisbury immediately spring to mind as particularly memorable instances where this has been carefully thought through, each in an entirely different way, so that all needs have been met. What resulted was an all embracing comprehensiveness of worship, with no threat to the role of the choir. It can be done.

6. With *the current shortage of organists*, and not even those available always wishing to be regularly involved every Sunday, some parishes have evolved a system whereby two or three organists do duty on a rota basis.

7. We need constantly to bear in mind that *where words fail, music can take over*. Because of the particular nature of music it is frequently more memorable than a sermon. This is not a cynical observation, though it makes the responsibility of the church musician the greater. Nevertheless, music must always serve, and never rule.

8. The work of the church musician will, at its best and most ideal, be directed towards *the concept of making all things new*, while recognizing that there are many things old and many things new which contribute towards that ideal treasure store.

9. There are so many opportunities open to us today *to enrich worship through music*. These we must willingly explore, grasp, and put into practice.

10. In these pages, I have often spoken of the need for flexibility and experimentation. At the same time I believe we have reached a point where, having experienced some years of liturgical change, *we now need a cooling off period* in order to create an essential stability, but in a way which will not ultimately create a further round of stagnation. As in the past, this could so easily result in the familiar providing a comfortable security. I believe there is a very real danger of this happening without our realizing it.

11. '*The greatest things are accomplished, and the greatest achievements won, by toil and by striving uninterrupted, toil as well of the body as of the spirit*'. These words of Richard Hakluyt the Elder seem to be as valid today as when he wrote them at the end of the sixteenth century. Hand in hand with this goes the constant need for encouragement, a commodity which all of us require in ample quantity, and which can be an antidote for some of the frustrations of today.

12. We live in an age where, generally speaking, many have never had it so good. It is a society where bigger and better material possessions are the order of the day, whether it be cars, refrigerators, steaks, holidays, or whatever. This becomes translated into church going where good music helps to draw people into church. In a similar way, badly performed music contributes towards driving some away from church. What a challenge – and what a responsibility – for the musicians.

QUESTIONS MARKS – AND FOOD FOR THOUGHT

1. *What are our attitudes to change?*
Are some of us content with things as they are? Do we know what we like, and like what we know, full stop? 'Change and decay in all around I see'. Do we sometimes automatically wish to equate change with decay?

Do we see tradition within the Church as a convenient cloak for leaving things as they are? ('As it was in the beginning, is now and ever shall be') or do we view tradition as something unchanging in a changing world? *All* change is as bad as *no* change.

Some time ago, the Duke of Edinburgh said to an American audience, 'If you think we in Britain are living in the past, forget it. We simply like to carry our history with us as we face an uncertain future'.

2. *The dangers of informality*, sometimes even an enforced matiness, can easily become a substitute for the transcendent and the numinous. In other words, are we sometimes encouraged to relegate the adoration and mystery of worship in favour of immediacy? Worship can surely be both transcendent and immanent, with the one complementing the other. Informality and excellence are not necessarily incompatible bed fellows.

3. I would suggest we need to consider ways and means of using *silence as an ingredient of worship*. The very nature of our new services with their many fragmentary

sections can all too easily produce a restlessness and sense of 'busyness' which, although it may reflect a certain aspect of worship, is not always conducive to prayer and meditation. Silence from music can be a welcome contrast, even a necessity.

The problem here lies in the nature of the secular world where silence is continually being assaulted by so much which devalues the use and sound of music. By the reverse token, silence in worship can so easily become a contrived nothingness, even to the extent of being an embarrassment simply because we do not know how to use it. Perhaps there is something we could learn to advantage from a study of the contemplative orders.

4. *On the practicalities of having a choir, or not.*

(a) Providing a choir makes musically acceptable sounds, there is no justification whatever for dispensing with it, however much some people might try to convince us otherwise. In any event, what would it be replaced by?

(b) Certain churches will, for one reason or another, be choirless (see pages 88–90). Because of the lack of resources there may be little hope of ever changing the situation and, in such circumstances, the role of the congregation needs to be carefully considered and suitably catered for.

(c) It will sometimes be that the parson will through default have to be the choirmaster, in which case the RSCM can offer advice and help on how to set about the task.

(d) There will inevitably be certain situations where a choir will be short of numbers. While local conditions, not least the availability of recruits, will contribute towards this, it is a reasonable assumption that a choir will be as good as the person in charge of it and that the charisma, or otherwise, of that person will in most instances determine in greater or lesser degree whether or not the choir stalls are full.

5. Whether a choir and its resources are fully used or are

underemployed are matters which need to be carefully thought through – and by all concerned. One of the laudable aspects of the Oxford Movement was to emphasize the role of music in worship. This in some instances unfortunately overspilt towards an excess of music with a virtual take-over bid, which today finds rather less acceptance than a generation ago.

WHAT OF THE FUTURE?

Gazing into the crystal ball must of necessity be speculative. But, all things being equal, there are certain pointers.

THE TRAINING OF THE CLERGY. I am utterly convinced that this, in terms of matters musical, is a priority and, moreover, that much of this must take place at theological college level. It is at this formulative and impressionable stage that ideas and opinions begin to be crystalized, and this as much through discussion with fellow students as through any other means. The need is not so much to be musical as to be fully informed, so as to enable one to act rationally and not impetuously.

I now pay regular visits to most of the theological colleges and find that some of the viewpoints expressed by the students, however sincerely motivated and thought through, are nevertheless born of ignorance as to the purpose and function of music in a worship situation. Add to this the possible element of rebellion, however benevolent, against the establishment and you have ingredients for some of the situations and impasses which can so easily arise. These can be the more traumatic when those concerned perhaps know they are unmusical and consequently give music a low rating in what they see as their priorities, or else admit no independent role for choirs and music.

THE MUSICIAN AND EDUCATION. I believe there is the need for a massive injection of new thinking here on the part of many church musicians. Nor is this by any means confined to amateurs. For some, there is an obsession with clinging, *de rigueur*, to the past with almost a death wish, resisting change at all costs, an attitude of mind many would never dream of subscribing to in their everyday life. Statements such as, 'I have no intention of coming to terms with the ASB', are convenient pegs on which to hang reluctance for coming to terms with anything which departs from the accustomed norm. Maybe this misapplied sense of nostalgia for 'the good old days' is evidence of an insecurity; but if we fail to inform ourselves, as a means towards educating others, we opt out of our responsibility as church musicians.

There is so much evidence of the new forms of services bringing new life that there is a real danger of those who think otherwise being ultimately left on the shelf as archaic and immovable relics. While there is no lasting future in jumping on to the popular bandwagon of change for change's sake, there is going to be even less future if we opt to live in a vacuum which sees the past as the only way forward. The course of world history has repeatedly shown what happens when such a course is adopted.

The nub of the matter is that some of us are far too engrossed in our own patch, and little more. The dangers of the resulting insularity of church musicians is quite contrary to the exploratory, inquisitive, sometimes even questioning nature of the world at large.

THE ATTITUDE OF MUSICIANS. One of the worst aspects of this wall of insularity erected by musicians is the closed mind attitude, which denies the necessity for help or improvement or for the injection of new thought identifying their work. Being apparently unaware of any musical shortcomings, they sometimes see no situation in need of being remedied, being in many instances far more concerned with acquainting all and sundry with their many years of service, or whatever. What is so sad is that, through a blinkered and frequently stubborn attitude, they fail to see that they alienate themselves from their clergy and congregations, sometimes even from their choirs, and certainly from the main stream.

In terms of the RSCM such situations are extremely frustrating, for these are the very people we ought to be helping; but they will not let us help, either because they are reticent to come forward or, worst of all, because they think they know all the answers. In the event, as with the clergy, it means that much of our work revolves around preaching to the converted.

THE NEED FOR FLEXIBILITY. If an ideal partnership is to prevail, clergy and musicians must be prepared to adjust willingly to every situation. In this, no two churches are likely to be similar. If worship itself is too circumscribed there is little prospect of the music being otherwise. If the musical situation is allowed to deteriorate, worship will similarly deteriorate. Such is the power of music either to enrich or to impoverish. These factors dictate that we must take music seriously. Against the present day background, especially that of the ASB, we cannot afford to do otherwise.

In the final analysis, whatever the situation and whatever the circumstances, from the ultra-conservative to the ultra-way out, and all that lies between these two extremes, one can only emphasize the need for doing all things well and that the cheap and tawdry should be no more acceptable in church than elsewhere. The completeness of our offering, so that worship can truly become the meeting place of earth and heaven, will without doubt be more nearly achieved through the enrichment which music uniquely offers; and this will be realized if we have vision, with one eye on the past, one eye on the present, but both eyes on the future.

What a challenge as we move forward into the twenty-first century. What a grand and glorious vision as the point of departure for what some would have us believe is the post-Christian era. We have a unique moment of opportunity to explore endless possibilities of musical adventure with a willing expansion of thought providing the springboard for this. How much better than the alternative of burying our heads in the sands and retracting.